The Power of Her Sympathy

The Power of Her Sympathy

The Autobiography and Journal of

Catharine Maria Sedgwick

Edited and with an Introduction by Mary Kelley

1993

BOSTON, MASSACHUSETTS

PUBLISHED BY THE MASSACHUSETTS HISTORICAL SOCIETY

DISTRIBUTED BY NORTHEASTERN UNIVERSITY PRESS · BOSTON

Library of Congress Cataloging-in-Publication Data

Sedgwick, Catharine Maria, 1789–1867.
  The power of her sympathy : the autobiography and journal of
Catharine Maria Sedgwick / edited and with an introduction by
Mary Kelley.
  Includes index.
  ISBN 0-934909-35-0 ISBN 0-934909-36-9 (soft cover)
  1. Sedgwick, Catharine Maria, 1798–1867—Biography.   2.
Sedgwick, Catharine Maria, 1789–1867—Diaries.   3. Women
novelists, American—19th century—Biography.   4. Women
novelists. American—20th century—Diaries.   I. Kelley, Mary.
1943-II. Title.
PS2798.Z5A36 1993
813'.2—dc20

Published at the charge of the Publication Fund

Designed by David Ford

FOR

Barbara Miller Solomon

SCHOLAR

MENTOR

FRIEND

IN MEMORIAM

Contents

Editorial Note

Catharine Maria Sedgwick's autobiography and journals are deposited at the Massachusetts Historical Society. Divided into two sections and dated 5 May 1853 and 10 March 1860, the two volumes of the autobiography were composed as a series of recollections for Alice Minot, the young daughter of Sedgwick's niece, Kate Sedgwick Minot. In these closely written volumes, Sedgwick focused upon her childhood and adolescence. Sedgwick also kept a journal throughout much of her adulthood. Carefully dated and bound in mottled paper, the journal's twelve volumes contain entries dating from the summer of 1821. Sedgwick made her final entry on 28 December 1854.

In preparing the autobiography's 163 pages of manuscript for publication, I have modernized the original spelling, capitalization, and punctuation. Capitals, periods, and commas have been supplied where needed to clarify Sedgwick's meaning. Ampersands have been rendered as "and," superscript letters lowered, abbreviations expanded, and obvious misspellings corrected. Words and phrases that I have conjectured as well as other editorial insertions have been placed within brackets. Canceled text has been omitted. Where appropriate, I have identified the individuals, events, and places mentioned in the text. I have also included extensive selections from the twelve volumes of the journal. The same editorial policies have been adopted for these selections.

Mary E. Dewey included portions of the autobiography in *The Life and Letters of Catharine M. Sedgwick,* a selection of Sedgwick's letters and journals published by Harper and Brothers in 1872. In editing the autobiography, Dewey abbreviated names, deleted sections, and changed the organization of the text. I have maintained the original throughout. Marginalia that Sedgwick marked as inserts have been incorporated. Selections from the journals have also been based on the original manuscripts.

Acknowledgments

Many people have made this volume a shared enterprise. My colleagues at Dartmouth College and elsewhere have long provided me with a remarkably expansive community that has sustained me, intellectually and personally. This project has been no exception. I am indebted to Carol Holly, Judith McGaw, Megan Marshall, Annelise Orleck, Nell Irvin Painter, Ivy Schweitzer, and Barbara Sicherman, all of whom brought their considerable talents to bear upon the introduction. Exceptional critic, equally exceptional stylist, Robert Eaton Kelley has made an imprint on these pages, as he has on my life.

Dartmouth College's support has been unfailingly generous. A Faculty Fellowship enabled me to begin research on this volume. The College's Presidential Scholars Program provided funding for research assistance. Whether they were developing bibliography, preparing information for the annotations, or reading page proof, Pherabe Kolb, Lynn Rainville, and Susannah Shin displayed abundant resourcefulness, keen analytical abilities, and good cheer. Students and faculty alike are deeply indebted to President James Freedman who initiated this Program. Always ready to meet inquiries no matter how obscure, Baker Library's Virginia Close demonstrated yet again her unrivaled talents.

The Massachusetts Historical Society, where the papers of Catharine Maria Sedgwick are housed, has sponsored this project. Director Louis Leonard Tucker's invitation to speak at an afternoon meeting of the Society set the stage. My lecture, and particularly my analysis of Sedgwick's autobiography and journals as a signal contribution to American letters, led to the idea for this volume. Peter Drummey, the Society's Librarian, has lightened many a task. Not least, he came to my aid at those moments when Sedgwick's closely written pages seemed undecipherable. Editor of Publications Conrad E. Wright has been this project's supporter from the outset. The meticulous care that he has taken with the manuscript has been invaluable, as has his editorial guidance at every stage of the process. During the weeks and then the months that I spent at the Massachusetts Historical Society, Helene and David Roberts provided me that very important room of my own. In this and in many ways, their generosity has been unparalleled.

There are many reasons that this volume is dedicated to Barbara Miller Solomon. Catharine Maria Sedgwick introduced us to each other nearly twenty years ago. Barbara was already a distinguished historian. I was a graduate student in the early stages of research on my dissertation. Seated across from each other at a table stacked with boxes of Sedgwick's papers, Barbara and I read her letters, diaries, and journals together. There was an almost immediate identification between us, an almost immediate sense of collaboration. Only later did I learn that nearly everyone so fortunate as to meet Barbara shared this experience. An historian of remarkable talent, Barbara was still more. For me and for so many others, she was an equally remarkable mentor. It was Barbara who initially taught me that the study of the past is a shared enterprise. From her I learned as well the meaning of commitment to the study of women's past. Blending passionate engagement with ready laughter, Barbara graced my life for two decades. In the last weeks before her death, she read this volume which stands as testament to her memory. She is now and will always be sorely missed.

Mary Kelley
Hanover, New Hampshire
July 1993

Introduction

In a letter written on 5 October 1851, Catharine Maria Sedgwick responded to a proposal made by William Minot, the husband of Sedgwick's beloved niece and namesake, Kate. William had suggested that Sedgwick, a nationally acclaimed author of novels, tales, and sketches, undertake her autobiography. Had William appealed to her on the basis of her literary achievements, this inveterately modest woman almost certainly would have declined. Not surprisingly, then, William asked that the autobiography be written for his and Kate's daughter Alice, a child to whom Sedgwick was devoted.

Nonetheless, the project seemed daunting. A woman who had remained unmarried despite the protestations of suitors, Sedgwick told William she had "'boarded round' so much, had my home in so many houses and so many hearts," indeed had her life "so woven into the fabric of others that I seem to have had no separate, individual existence." Nowhere else in the entire body of Sedgwick's writings did she reveal more about the character of her richly textured relationships with her parents, her brothers and sisters, her nieces and nephews. Nowhere else did she signal more strikingly the impact those relationships had had upon her sense of self. Ironically, this conception of herself as intertwined with the lives of those whom she cherished also meant that she would not refuse William's request, that she would consider it her "filial duty." Telling him that "perhaps I might tell a short and pleasant story to my darling Alice," Sedgwick displayed her typical modesty. Just as typically, she achieved much more than she promised in her autobiography of a childhood and adolescence that had spanned the opening years of the early republic. Gathering together the threads of memory, Sedgwick wove together a deeply personal narrative with an illuminating portrayal of a newly independent America.[1]

Sedgwick also kept a journal throughout much of her adulthood. Beginning with entries that she made in the summer of 1821 when she was thirty-one, Sedgwick filled twelve volumes with medita-

[1]Catharine Maria Sedgwick to William Minot, 5 Oct. 1851, Catharine Maria Sedgwick Papers, Massachusetts Historical Society.

tions upon the author as an adult and the world she shared with other antebellum Americans. Taken together, the autobiography and the journals constitute her self-representation, child to adult. No less they offer readers a representation of both the changes and the continuities characterizing relations of power in the decades between America's Revolution and its Civil War. More than a century before historians did so, Sedgwick situated power in its broadest context. Her autobiography and journal extended the meaning of power to include gender relations as a central dimension. They addressed with equal insight social and political relations.

Ranked with Washington Irving, James Fenimore Cooper, and William Cullen Bryant as a founder of her nation's literature, Sedgwick published six novels and nearly one hundred tales and sketches in a career that spanned the four decades before the Civil War. Ranging from a revisionary portrayal of the conflict between Puritans and Indians to a dissection of a Jacksonian America dominated by commercialism, Sedgwick's fiction also dealt with issues that were decidedly social and political in character. Portrayals of reform movements, discourses on class relations, doctrinal debates between Congregationalists and Unitarians, all these issues and more were interwoven in a body of literature that spoke to the felt realities of early nineteenth-century Americans. Equally concerned with issues of gender, Sedgwick placed strong, independent, and articulate heroines at the center of her fiction. Sedgwick's model of gender relations presumed different roles for women and men. Nonetheless, she accorded women signal status as central social and cultural actors.

In the opening sentence of her autobiography, Sedgwick described the project as a collection of "memories."[2] Begun in the sixty-fourth year of her life, Sedgwick's autobiography was in the narrowest sense exactly that—a commemorative text designed to

---

[2] Autobiography of Catharine Maria Sedgwick, Catharine Maria Sedgwick Papers, Massachusetts Historical Society. Unless otherwise noted, all subsequent references derive from this source.

inscribe the past upon the present. However, the design, the effort "to brighten the links of the chain that binds us to those who have gone before, and to keep it fast and strong" had significance beyond this objective. Perhaps most important, Sedgwick departed from an autobiographical tradition in which the self moved inexorably toward separation and individuation. In sanctioning connection, in stressing reciprocal commitment, Sedgwick stood in contrast to other notable American autobiographers such as Benjamin Franklin, Ralph Waldo Emerson, and Henry Adams, each of whom presented the self on a trajectory toward autonomy.[3] Sedgwick's emphasis upon an identity constructed in relation to others located her narrative in an alternative tradition initiated by the fourteenth-century Englishwoman Dame Julian of Norwich. Julian's *Revelations*, Margery Kempe's fifteenth-century *Book of Margery Kempe*, and Margaret Cavendish's *True Relation* two centuries later all defined the self in relation to others. New Englander Anne Bradstreet inscribed the same relational self in her seventeenth-century "To

[3] This perspective was set forth in Georges Gusdorf, "Conditions and Limits of Autobiography," an influential essay published in 1956. Autobiography, as Gusdorf has defined it, entails a "conscious awareness of the singularity of each individual life" (30). Whatever its merits for analysis of the male autobiographical self, Gusdorf's theory is based solely upon analysis of men's experiences. See James Olney's translation of the essay in Olney, ed., *Autobiography: Essays Theoretical and Critical* (Princeton, 1980), 28–48. Susan Stanford Friedman has highlighted the gendered character of this individualistic theory in "Women's Autobiographical Selves: Theory and Practice." See Shari Benstock, ed., *The Private Self: Theory and Practice of Women's Autobiographical Writings* (Chapel Hill, 1988), 34–62. Until recently, scholarship on autobiography has focused almost exclusively on male texts. As her title suggests, Sidonie Smith's *A Poetics of Women's Autobiography: Marginality and the Fictions of Self-Representation* (Bloomington, 1987), shifts the angle of vision. I have found Smith's commentary on current theories of women's autobiography very useful. See also Estelle Jelinek, *The Tradition of Women's Autobiography: From Antiquity to the Present* (Boston, 1986); Carolyn Heilbrun, *Writing a Woman's Life* (New York, 1988); Personal Narratives Group, eds., *Interpreting Women's Lives: Feminist Theory and Personal Narratives* (Bloomington, 1989); Margo Cully, ed., *American Women's Autobiography: Fea(s)ts of Memory* (Madison, 1992). For commentary on the varied forms of life writing, including letters, journals, and autobiographies analyzed in this introduction, see Susan Groag Bell and Marilyn Yalom, eds. *Revealing Lives: Autobiography, Biography, and Gender* (Albany, 1990), 1–11.

My Dear Children." So too did Sedgwick in the middle of the nine-teenth century.[4]

Just as the self that Sedgwick presented to Alice had taken its shape from the individual circumstances of her life and the larger social and cultural milieu of early nineteenth-century America, so Sedgwick herself shaped those sources in the presentation of her childhood and adolescence.[5] Born in Stockbridge, Massachusetts, on 28 December 1789, Catharine Maria was the third daughter and sixth child of Theodore and Pamela Dwight Sedgwick. Descended from one of the most distinguished families in the Connecticut River Valley, Pamela Dwight married Theodore Sedgwick in 1774. She had chosen a husband who rapidly achieved the standing of her parents, the socially prominent Joseph and Abigail Dwight. Theo-dore's election to both houses of the Massachusetts legislature made the Sedgwicks a leading family in the state prior to their daughter's birth. The next decade brought national distinction. Elected to the United States House of Representatives, in which he served as speaker, and the Senate, Theodore became one of the early repub-lic's most influential Federalists. His proud daughter recalled that Theodore and his allies in the "Federal party loved their country, and were devoted to it, as virtuous parents are to their children."

However much these powerful Federalists may have been dedi-cated to their nation, they found their claims to leadership in a newly independent America challenged by those who sought a

---

[4]In her analysis of the autobiographies of Dame Julian of Norwich, Margery Kempe, Margaret Cavendish, and Anne Bradstreet, Mary Mason has highlighted characteristics that distinguish women's from men's construction of the self. See "The Other Voice: Autobiographies of Women Writers" in Olney, ed., *Autobiography*, 207–235. Carol Holly has employed a similar strategy in analyzing the autobiographies of Sedgwick and Lucy Larcom. See "Nineteenth-Century Autobiographies of Affiliation: The Case of Catha-rine Sedgwick and Lucy Larcom" in Paul John Eakin, ed., *American Autobiography: Retrospect and Prospect* (Madison, 1991), 216–234. See also Rose Norman, "New England Girlhoods in Nineteenth-Century Autobiography," *Legacy: A Journal of American Women Writers* 8(1991):104–117.

[5]Sidonie Smith has explored the complicated relationship between experience and representation in women's autobiography in the highly suggestive "Construing Truths in Lying Mouths: Truthtelling in Women's Autobiography," *Studies in the Literary Imag-ination* 23(1990):145–163.

more egalitarian society. The hierarchy, the finely graded stratification, and the deference to a gentlemanly elite that had prevailed in colonial society no longer seemed secure.[6] In the description of her mother's parents, Sedgwick illustrated the contrast between that earlier world and the one being born in the years following the American Revolution. A "gentleman par excellence of his time," Joseph Dwight had been a highly successful lawyer and land speculator in the Connecticut River Valley. One of Stockbridge's prominent residents and trustee of its Indian school, Joseph's status had been conveyed to posterity in a painting that displayed his "most delicately beautiful hands." Sedgwick presumed that her grandfather had simply wanted to show his descendants that he "had kept 'clean hands,' a commendable virtue, physically or morally speaking." Perhaps he did, but those hands had had a more immediate purpose for Joseph, serving as an emblem of the divide separating a member of the elite from the rest of his contemporaries. Virtually everything about Abigail Dwight had performed the same service. Described in terms of readily identifiable signifiers of status, the woman who shared in the management of the Indian school was "dignified," "benevolent," and "pleasing." Like the hands that her husband displayed, the apparel that Abigail donned confirmed her social standing. The "dress, of rich silk, a high-crowned cap, with plaited border, and a watch, then so seldom worn as to be a distinction, all marked the gentlewoman, and inspired respect."

In the midst of a transformation that was altering their nation's social and political premises, a postrevolutionary elite continued to defend the prerogatives that had set Joseph and Abigail apart. However, the markers that Sedgwick described in her autobiography were now subject to challenge. Infuriated that forms of deference signifying a hierarchical society were being cast aside, Theo-

---

[6]The unparalleled social and political changes that occurred in the decades following the Revolution are insightfully explored in Gordon S. Wood, "The Democratization of Mind in the American Revolution," in *Leadership in the American Revolution, Papers Presented at the Third Symposium, May 9 and 10, 1974* (Washington, 1974), 63–89. These changes have received extended treatment in Wood's recently published *The Radicalism of the American Revolution* (New York, 1992).

dore Sedgwick's brow had lowered when emboldened artisans presented themselves at the *front* door of his home. He did more than glower when a still more presumptuous representative of the coming order stood at the same door and refused to remove his hat. The lad had been forcibly removed by the elder Sedgwick, albeit with the hat still securely on his head. Clearly, as his daughter remarked wryly, Theodore had been "born too soon to relish the freedoms of democracy." The same might be said for Pamela Sedgwick. She had insisted that the family and the servants be segregated—household help, Catharine recalled, had been "restricted to the kitchen table." Sedgwick's recollections documented the increasing resistance to Pamela's practice. "Now Cath*arine*," said a local resident when the young Sedgwick had been sent to recruit the woman's daughter for a servant, "we are all made out of the same clay, we have got one Maker and one Judge, and we've got to lay down in the grave side by side. Why can't you sit down to the table together."

The conflict between those defending the older order and their challengers took on a political cast in the competition between the nation's parties, the Federalists and the Democratic-Republicans.[7] The political philosophy of loyal Federalist Theodore bore all the marks of a party committed to the maintenance of a traditional hierarchy—a paternalistic approach to politics, a belief that only elite leadership could sustain the nation, and a haughty distrust of the lower orders. Theodore's commitment to the republican experiment was not the issue. Service as a legislator in the Massachusetts General Court, leadership in the nation's Congress, and tenure on the Massachusetts Supreme Court all testified to his dedication to republican government founded under the Constitution. Instead, it

[7]The conduct and character of Massachusetts politics are described in Ronald P. Formisano, *The Transformation of Political Culture: Massachusetts Parties, 1790s-1840s* (New York, 1983). The Federalists are analyzed in James M. Banner, Jr., *To the Hartford Convention: The Federalists and the Origins of Party Politics in Massachusetts, 1789–1815* (New York, 1970). Paul Goodman does the same for the opposition in *The Democratic-Republicans of Massachusetts: Politics in a Young Republic* (Cambridge, Mass., 1964). See also Linda K. Kerber's analysis of the Federalist ideology in *Federalists in Dissent: Imagery and Ideology in Jeffersonian America* (Ithaca, 1970).

was the very meaning of republicanism that was being contested during the three decades of Theodore's career. Sedgwick recalled that her father and other prominent Federalists "hoped a republic might exist and prosper." Indeed, they entertained the hope that it might "be the happiest government in the world, but not without a strong aristocratic element." It was that last reservation, that insistence upon a "strong aristocratic element," that separated leading Federalists from those dedicated to a republicanism in which all of the enfranchised played a role in the conduct of politics.

The Federalists' opposition to increased popular participation was informed by their allegiance to a traditional social structure that divided the world into gentlemen and lower orders. Men like Theodore who identified "all sound principles, truth, justice, and patriotism" with a gentlemanly elite had no truck with the lower orders, at least as political entities. They, as Sedgwick recalled, were dismissed by her father "as 'Jacobins,' 'sans culottes,' and 'miscreants.'" Theodore's epithets notwithstanding, he surely recognized, as his daughter did, that the forces opposing him possessed an "intense desire to grasp the power and place that had been denied to them, and a determination to work out the theories of the government." With the election of 1800 Theodore believed they had accomplished exactly that. The defeat of his party at the polls and the rejection of the republicanism with which he identified led Theodore to resign his Congressional seat. Still in control of Massachusetts, the Federalists appointed him to the state's highest court. Disillusioned but still eager to wield influence, he remained there until his death in 1813.

Despite the highly publicized hostility between the rival parties, Theodore's daughter suggested that politics had a lighter side. And despite Theodore's sober sense of purpose, his daughter caught the pranks, the lampoons, and the unpretentious humor of the times. She recorded these memories in her autobiography. They also became the subject of "A Reminiscence of Federalism," a story Sedgwick based upon a summer she spent in Bennington, Vermont, during the last decade of the eighteenth century. Bennington's main street, as she noted in the autobiography, "extended a long way, some mile and a half, from a hill at one end to a plain at the other." It was there that the village's residents were likely to find Clover, an old horse who had been left to graze. Clover was no ordinary horse. His distinction was that his superannuated sides had been "pasted over with lampoons in which the rival factions vented their wit or their malignity safe from personal responsibility, for Clover could tell no tales." Daily, indeed hourly, Clover "trudged from the hill, a walking gazette, his ragged and grizzled sides covered with the militant missives, and returned bearing the responses of the valley, as unconscious of his hostile burden, as the mail is of its portentous contents." In her story, which she published in 1835, Sedgwick allows one Democratic-Republican to voice his opinion that "distrust of the people was the great error of the Federalists"; the narrator responds that that perspective "will now perhaps be admitted with truth."[8] Sedgwick had come to the same opinion only with adulthood. The younger Sedgwick, as she readily admitted in her autobiography, had aligned herself with her father, looking upon every member of the opposition as "grasping, dishonest, and vulgar." Every member of the rival party had been cast as "an enemy to his country."

The hierarchy and deference under assault in the social and political relations of the early republic had also characterized gender relations in colonial society. Whether gentlewoman or member of the lower orders, a woman had been considered a man's subordinate. In a hierarchy that divided the world into the feminine and the masculine, a woman had been expected to defer to male authority in the household and in the world beyond its doors. Many of the underpinnings of this system remained intact in the years after the Revolution. Women were still subject to coverture, a legal tradition that submerged a wife's property in her husband's. They were still denied participation in the nation's body politic either as voters

---

[8]Catharine Maria Sedgwick, "A Reminiscence of Federalism," in *Tales and Sketches* (Philadelphia, 1835), 24, 30.

or as jurors. Simultaneously, however, subtle but discernible changes were becoming evident. Enhanced opportunities for female education began to erase the disparity in literacy between white women and white men. Building upon the basic literacy taught in public schools, an increasing number of private academies and seminaries provided women a more extended and diversified education. Republican motherhood, an ideology that ascribed political significance to domestic responsibilities, made women's education critical to the survival of the newly independent nation. Expected to foster the necessary elements of virtue in their sons and to encourage the same in their husbands, mothers and wives became the educators of their nation's citizens. In fulfilling this obligation, women participated, albeit indirectly, in civil and political life. Standing as an archetype of gender relations, the institution of marriage registered continuity and change in the early republic. Women did remain subject to the intersecting strands of subordination and authority that had marked colonial marriages. Nonetheless, the practice of more egalitarian relations in some households signaled modifications in this pattern. Not least, the idea that a woman might remain unmarried and still have a meaningful life was glimpsed as a possibility. Within a generation, Catharine Maria Sedgwick counted herself among the women who made that idea a reality.[9]

---

[9]There is now a considerable body of scholarship that examines the Revolution in relation to women. Linda Kerber has written extensively on the Revolution's legal and political implications. She also identified Republican Motherhood in her pathbreaking article "The Republican Mother: Women and the Enlightenment—An American Perspective," *American Quarterly* 28(1976):187–205. See also Rosemarie Zagarri, "Morals, Manners, and the Republican Mother," *American Quarterly* 44(1992):192–215. Jan Lewis commented upon a republican wife's responsibility to her husband in "The Republican Wife: Virtue and Seduction in the Early Republic," *William and Mary Quarterly*, 3rd ser., 44(1987):696–721. Both Kerber and Mary Beth Norton have addressed the significance of women's increased educational opportunities. More recently, I have done the same in "'Vindicating the Equality of Female Intellect': Women and Authority in the Early Republic," *Prospects: An Annual Journal of American Cultural Studies* 17(1992):1–27. Norton suggested that the choice to remain unmarried became viable in the years after the Revolution. See Kerber, *Women of the Republic: Intellect and Ideology in Revolutionary America* (Chapel Hill, 1980); "The Paradox of Women's Citizenship in the

The marriages of Theodore Sedgwick illustrated the persistence of older patterns of gender relations. Before he had reached the age of twenty-eight, Theodore had married twice, enhancing his status both times. His marriage to Eliza Mason, a member of a prominent family in Franklin, Connecticut, was crossed by tragedy. When he contracted smallpox three years after their marriage, Theodore immediately removed himself from the household and returned only after he had been certified as recovered. These precautions notwithstanding, Eliza, whose pregnancy had made inoculation inadvisable, became infected. The smallpox that her husband had barely survived killed her. Although Sedgwick believed that only "the canonized 'year and a day'" had elapsed before her parents' marriage, Theodore actually married Pamela Dwight in 1774, three years after Eliza's death. Whatever their individual differences, Eliza and Pamela both practiced the deference toward Theodore that traditional gender relations mandated. And, as if to signify the wifely role she and Eliza shared, Pamela enshrined the memory of her predecessor in the name of her eldest child, Eliza Mason.

In characterizing her mother as "modest," "humble," and "reserved," Sedgwick described the posture that Pamela adopted toward her husband. The negotiations between Pamela and Theodore when the latter was deciding whether to continue his political career are illustrative. In a letter that Sedgwick included in the autobiography, Pamela suggested that her husband consider the toll exacted by his career. Telling Theodore in the latter part of the 1780s that "a wish to serve the true interests of our country is certainly a laudable ambition," she immediately added that "the intention brings many cares with it." With a striking ease and confidence, she commented on the political realities that her husband faced in the waning years of the eighteenth century—the government was as yet untried, the citizenry as yet untested. However, both the ease and confidence disappeared when she came to the costs that mattered

---

Early Republic: The Case of Martin vs. Massachusetts, 1805," *American Historical Review* 97(1992):349–378; Norton, *Liberty's Daughters: The Revolutionary Experience of American Women, 1750-1800* (Boston, 1980).

most to her. She could say only hesitantly that "your family deserves some attention." She could not say at all that *she* merited consideration: "I have not a distant wish you should sacrifice your happiness to mine, or your inclination to my opinion." Instead, should Theodore decide to continue to pursue a career that took him away from his family at least half of each year, Pamela duly assured him that "submission is my duty, and, however hard, I will try to practice what reason teaches me I am under obligation to do." At the top of the letter, which was deposited with the family's correspondence at the Massachusetts Historical Society, Sedgwick wrote in her own hand: "a beautiful and characteristic letter from my beloved mother, wise and tender."[10]

Her daughter's sentiments notwithstanding, Pamela found the separations from her husband very hard indeed. Sedgwick herself acknowledged that her mother had been "left for many months in this cold northern country, with young children, a large household, and complicated concerns, and the necessity of economy." Pamela's letters to her husband focused upon the isolation, the longing for companionship, that made the separations still more difficult. Indeed, her letters were a litany of loneliness. Theodore's departure occasioned a "very sensible pain," although she had tried to conceal it so as not to distress him. Disappointed that his return was delayed yet again, she told him in another letter: "I sicken at the thought of your being absent for so long a time." She found almost intolerable "this vale of Widowhood." Perhaps most tellingly, Pamela confided in still another letter, "we are all like a body without a soul."[11]

The costs of separation increased as Pamela's already fragile health became more precarious and her struggle with depression more desperate. In December 1791, she pleaded with her husband to return home and the next moment ordered him to stay away. The letter was short. It told Theodore that she had sunk deeply into

[10]Pamela Dwight Sedgwick to Theodore Sedgwick, 18 Nov. [179?], Sedgwick IV, Massachusetts Historical Society.

[11]Pamela Dwight Sedgwick to Theodore Sedgwick, 31 Jan. 1789, 26 June 1790, 14 Feb. 1791, Sedgwick III, Massachusetts Historical Society.

herself. Friends had tried to tell her that she was ill, "but this I have no reason to believe." Yet as the words tumbled from her pen she made Theodore believe: "But shall I tell, can I tell you that I have lost my understanding." What was she to think, what could she think, she wondered, "what is my shame, what is my pain, what is my confusion to think of this what evils [a]wait my poor family without a guide, without a head." She wanted him to return for the children, "for their sakes," but surely not for his or for hers, "for your sake I wish you not to come, you must not come. It would only make us both more wretched."[12] Although Pamela rallied from that attack, others that followed were still more severe. In a letter that Sedgwick included in her autobiography, Theodore told his other daughters, Eliza and Frances, that as Pamela's condition deteriorated, he had struggled to decide whether to remain in Congress or resign his office: "I most sincerely endeavored to weigh all circumstances, and to discover what I ought to do." Theodore continued his career. Pamela continued to suffer increasingly serious attacks of depression until her death in 1807.

Ostensibly, Sedgwick defended her father's decision, declaring in the autobiography that Theodore's letters had been filled with the "most thoughtful love for my mother, the highest appreciation of her character." Claiming that only devotion to his country had made him persist in his career, Sedgwick stressed that her father had "felt it to be his duty to remain in public life at every private sacrifice." Perhaps most important, Pamela's suffering had ended with her death. And his daughter insisted, Theodore's contribution "to establish the government, and to swell the amount of that political virtue which makes the history of the Federal party the record of the purest patriotism the world has known—*that remains.*"

Simultaneously, however, Sedgwick subverted this defense of her father. In some of the most moving passages in the autobiography, she tallied the costs of Theodore's choice. Surely the largest toll had

---

[12]Pamela Dwight Sedgwick to Theodore Sedgwick, 4 Dec. 1791, Sedgwick III, Massachusetts Historical Society.

been exacted from Pamela. Acknowledging the pain her mother had suffered, Sedgwick noted that the separations seemed "to have been almost cruel to her." She had been "oppressed with cares and responsibilities." She had borne the "terrible weight of domestic cares." But Sedgwick did not stop there. The daughter also exposed her own deeply ambivalent response. She also had her litany. There was the recollection of her initial words as a child, "Theodore" and "Philadelphia"—words that signified the felt reality of her father's absence. There was the deliberate linkage of childhood's sorrows and joys with "Papa's going away," and "Papa's coming home." There was the impassioned statement about the suffering she had endured at the time of Pamela's death. "Beloved mother," she exclaimed, "even at this distance of time, the thought of what I suffered when you died thrills my soul!" And there was the decision to include the wrenchingly powerful eulogy. Penned by her brother Harry shortly after Pamela's death, it testified to their mother's endurance. Declaring that "her sufferings, in degree and duration, have been perhaps without a parallel," Harry emphasized that she had nonetheless displayed "the invincible meekness and the gentleness of her heavenly temper." Meekness, gentleness, in a word, subordination highlighted the gender relations that Pamela practiced. It was the costs inherent in those relations that led Sedgwick to undermine the defense of her father. Unable to elide the evidence of her ambivalence, Theodore's and Pamela's daughter scattered its traces through the text of her autobiography.

Theodore's absence and Pamela's illness obliged Catharine to look elsewhere for daily care, support, and guidance. She found all that and more in Elizabeth Freeman, an African American who was the family's servant for twenty-six years. In the passage in the autobiography that described "Mah Bet," or Mumbet, Sedgwick remarked to Alice that those "who surround us in our childhood, whose atmosphere infolds us, as it were, have more to do with the formation of our characters than all our didactic and preceptive education." It was Mumbet's "perception of justice," her "uncompromising honesty," her "conduct of high intelligence" that had left an indelible impression on Theodore's and Pamela's daughter. When Sedgwick described my "'Mother'—my nurse—my faithful friend" in a volume of her journal, she recorded that same impression. In an entry made only a month before Mumbet's death on 28 December 1829, Sedgwick mentioned the "strong love of justice," the "incorruptible integrity," and the "intelligent industry," all of which she later noted in her autobiography. The characteristics highlighted in her journal also suggested exceptional strength, determination, and force. Mumbet exhibited "strong judgment," she had "iron resolution," she demonstrated "quick and firm decision." Embodying a power that set her apart from other individuals in the autobiography and the journal, Mumbet emerged as the most exceptional individual, regardless of sex. Still more tellingly, she emerged as the woman with whom Sedgwick most deeply identified, and, in turn, Sedgwick declared, Mumbet had "clung to us with a devotion and tenacity of love seldom equalled."[13]

Significantly, however, Sedgwick was oblivious to the structural limitations of her relationship with the beloved Mumbet. The individual that Sedgwick inscribed in the autobiography and the journals appeared as an icon. Presented as if untouched by the disabilities of the racially based institution of slavery that dominated late eighteenth-century America, the loyal servant was constructed exclusively in relation to Sedgwick and her family. It was almost as if the racial difference between Mumbet and Sedgwick, between black and white, was erased. Notwithstanding Sedgwick's devotion, racial difference privileged Sedgwick and made Mumbet her subordinate.[14]

Mumbet was simultaneously Elizabeth Freeman, the African American who had challenged slavery's legality in the newly inde-

[13]Journal of Catharine Maria Sedgwick, 29 Nov. 1829, Catharine Maria Sedgwick Papers, Massachusetts Historical Society. See entry pp. 125–126.
[14]In her illuminating essay on the neglected dimensions of difference, Elsa Barkley Brown has analyzed the relational character of difference. See "'What Has Happened Here': The Politics of Difference in Women's History and Feminist Politics," *Feminist Studies* 18(1992):295–312. See also Nell Irvin Painter's introduction to *The Secret Eye: The Journal of Ella Gertrude Clanton Thomas, 1848–1889* (Chapel Hill, 1990), 1–67.

pendent state of Massachusetts. It is Freeman whom Sedgwick celebrated in "Slavery in New England," a chronicle of one African
American's struggle for freedom that she published in *Bentley's Miscellany* in 1853. Here Sedgwick acknowledged the difference between
herself and Mumbet. Here too she inscribed Mumbet with agency.
Having decided that the Declaration of Independence applied to all
Americans, the slave Freeman had approached Theodore Sedgwick
early in 1781. "Won't the law give me my freedom?" she had asked
Berkshire County's most prominent lawyer. After Freeman enlisted
Theodore as her counsel and challenged the constitutionality of
slavery in the county's court, the law did exactly that. Freeman's
achievement of freedom established a precedent for slavery's abolition throughout Massachusetts. Immediately after the court's decision, Freeman joined the Sedgwicks as the family's servant. It was
Mumbet's personal strength, her determination, her force, all of
which had been highlighted in the autobiography and journal that
made possible *Freeman's* public pursuit of liberation, an act that
Sedgwick applauded in "Slavery in New England."[15]

Sedgwick's older siblings also played an influential role in her
childhood. Deeply attached to all of her brothers and sisters, Sedgwick developed the strongest ties with her four brothers, Theodore,
Harry, Robert, and Charles. Sharing with them "an intimate companionship and I think as true and loving a friendship as ever existed between brothers and sister," she considered them her
"chiefest blessing in life." Long after her childhood had ended, Sedgwick told a friend that she had "no recollection beyond the time

---

[15]Catharine Maria Sedgwick, "Slavery in New England," *Bentley's Miscellany*
34(1853):417–424. Freeman's challenge to the constitutionality of slavery is the subject
of Elaine MacEacheren, "Emancipation of Slavery in Massachusetts: A Reexamination,
1770-1790," *Journal of Negro History* 55(1970):289–306. See also Arthur Zilversmit,
"Quok Walker, Mumbet, and the Abolition of Slavery in Massachusetts," *William and
Mary Quarterly*, 3rd ser., 25(1968):614–624; John D. Cushing, "The Cushing Court and
the Abolition of Slavery in Massachusetts: More Notes on the Quok Walker Case,"
American Journal of Legal History 5(1961):118–144: and William O'Brien, "Did the Jenni-
son Case Outlaw Slavery in Massachusetts," *William and Mary Quarterly*, 3rd ser.,
17(1960): 219–241.

when they made my happiness."[16] Nearly a decade older and already away at school and college, Theodore had little impact on his sister's early years. However, the other brothers were a signal presence. Harry's "loving, generous disposition," his "domestic affections," strongly impressed his sister. Robert, designated as her "favorite," served as "protector and companion." And Charles, born two years after Sedgwick, "was the youngest of the family, and so held that peculiar relation to us all as junior." That status made him no less beloved. Charles, as Sedgwick made clear in her autobiography and journal, was "a joy and thanksgiving to me."

Born fourteen and eleven years before their younger sister, Eliza and Frances had a less decisive influence upon Sedgwick's childhood. Both, as she recalled, "were just at that period when girls' eyes are dazzled with their own glowing future." That future was marriage, of course. And it was the relationship between marital union and sibling separation which Sedgwick remembered about her sisters. In describing Eliza and Frances, Sedgwick focused upon the separation occasioned by the marriage of the eldest sister. The ceremony that might have been regarded as celebration of a newly formed union left the seven-year-old Sedgwick with "the impression that a wedding was rather a sundering than a forming of ties." Deeply upset at the prospect of separation from a sister who had played a maternal role in her early childhood, Sedgwick had cried at the wedding and had been taken away. Mumbet had tried to calm her, whispering "her 'hush' but for the first time it was impotent." Later the bridegroom, Thaddeus Pomeroy, had come to her and, trying to soothe her, had said, "Your sister may stay with you this summer!" Five decades later, Sedgwick had not forgotten her reaction: "*May!* How my whole being revolted at the word. He had the power to bind or loose my sister!" The significance of this incident cannot be lost on readers of the autobiography. Only two pages

---

[16]Catharine Maria Sedgwick to Orville Dewey, 7 Sept. 1841, in Mary E. Dewey, ed., *Life and Letters of Catharine M. Sedgwick* (New York, 1872), 278.

after she penned this impassioned statement, Sedgwick repeated it almost verbatim in a second description of the event.

Both status and gender determined the education that Theodore and Pamela Sedgwick provided their children. Theodore, Harry, Robert, and Charles were all sent to preparatory schools that trained them in the classical languages, then the basic requirement for higher education. With the exception of Charles, the brothers all attended college before they began their apprenticeships as lawyers. These opportunities marked them as sons of an elite family. Less than one percent of the male population attended institutions of higher learning as late as 1840. None of the female population did so, at least in the eighteenth century. Oberlin, which did welcome women, did not open its doors until 1832.[17] The family's standing also shaped the instruction offered Eliza, Frances, and Catharine, each of whom was provided the most advanced education then available to women: they attended a series of private schools in New York City, Albany, and Boston, where their programs combined a smattering of academic schooling with social accomplishments.[18]

Sedgwick herself sharply distinguished between her formal and informal education. Her "school life," she stated bluntly in her autobiography, "was a waste, my home life my only education." This disclaimer notwithstanding, she did receive the formal schooling

[17]Maris Vinovskis and Richard Bernard have demonstrated that only a tiny percentage of the population attended college before the Civil War. Basing their findings on federal censuses, they show that 0.8% were enrolled in 1840, 0.8% in 1850, and 1.0 % in 1860. See Vinovskis and Bernard, "Beyond Catharine Beecher: Female Education in the Antebellum Period," *Signs: Journal of Women in Culture and Society* 3(1978):859. Lawrence Cremin addresses education more generally in *American Education: The Colonial Experience, 1607–1783* (New York, 1970). Imaginative in approach and convincing in argument, Cremin's volume nonetheless suffers from a failure to distinguish between education offered females and males. Only the latter receive extensive consideration.

[18]Women's education is the subject of Thomas Woody, *A History of Women's Education in the United States* (New York, 1929). Published more than 50 years ago, Woody's two volumes remain the basic source, although they are more descriptive than analytic. Barbara Miller Solomon's insightful study, *In the Company of Educated Women: A History of Women and Higher Education in America* (New Haven, 1985), focuses upon higher education.

considered appropriate for the daughter of an elite family. Having sent Sedgwick to the local school in rural Stockbridge, Theodore and Pamela sought other opportunities for their daughter. When Sedgwick was eight, Pamela wrote to Theodore that she had sent Catharine to Bennington, Vermont, "as our school here is worse than none."[19] The daughter's letters to Theodore suggest that this was at least slightly exaggerated. But in the autobiography Sedgwick did say that if there was "any other school a little more select or better chanced, I went to that." Whatever the particular school, she noted wryly "our minds were not weakened by too much study." The demands were relatively insignificant and the curricula restricted to reading, spelling, geography, and arithmetic.

The family then enrolled their daughter in a series of schools in three different cities. Here, too, Catharine found the challenges slight. Recalling her experience in New York City with a mixture of levity and regret, she noted that as early as the age of eleven she had been sent there and "had the very best teaching of an eminent Professor of Dancing!" Her schooling at Mrs. Bell's in Albany continued in like fashion. Sedgwick recalled that Mrs. Bell herself "rose late, was half the time out of her school, and did very little when in it." Considering the instruction she offered when there, that may not have been a serious loss. In a letter written to her mother on 6 October 1803, the thirteen-year-old Sedgwick noted that she had "begun another piece of embroidery, a landscape. It has a very cultivated and rather a romantic appearance." But the daughter had begun to take a stand regarding the relative merits of her education. Little time would be devoted to embroidery in the future, she told her mother. The study of geography and the practice of writing were much more important.[20] So too was the mastery of a foreign language. In 1804, four years after she had begun French while in New York City, Sedgwick wrote to each parent describing her prog-

---

[19]Pamela Sedgwick to Theodore Sedgwick, 9 July 1798, Sedgwick III, Massachusetts Historical Society.

[20]Catharine Maria Sedgwick to Pamela Sedgwick, 6 Oct. 1803, Sedgwick IV, Massachusetts Historical Society.

ress at Mrs. Payne's in Boston. In November she told Pamela that she was "very well contented and pleased with my new situation" and that she was pleased as well with her French instructor, "a very excellent one, I assure you."[21] Nearly two months later, on the day after her fifteenth birthday, she answered Theodore's inquiry about her progress in French: "I hardly find time to attend to anything else; I am very fond of it and it is *my opinion* that I come on very well."[22] Nonetheless, the cumulative experience was judged inadequate and years later Sedgwick registered her intense and lasting disappointment in the autobiography: "I have all my life felt the want of more systematic training."

Although it was equally unsystematic, Sedgwick regarded her informal education far more positively. Noting that her father and her brothers had "uncommon mental vigor," she emphasized that "their daily habits, and pursuits, and pleasures were intellectual, and I naturally imbibed from them a kindred taste." Sedgwick paid particular tribute to her father, who read aloud to the family. She remembered listening at the age of eight to passages from Cervantes, Shakespeare, and Hume. The father who read aloud also pressed the daughter to read to herself. Telling her that he hoped she would "find it in your power to devote your mornings to reading," he reminded Sedgwick that hers was a privileged position— "there are few who can make such improvements by it and it would be to be lamented if this precious time should be lost."[23] Sedgwick heeded his counsel. Indeed, the "love of reading" that her father had instilled in her became to her "education." By the age of eleven, she was reading constantly, "chiefly novels." When she was twelve, Sedgwick added Rollin's multi-volume *Ancient History,* which introduced her to "Cyrus's greatness." Lighter fare included the in-

---

[21]Catharine Maria Sedgwick to Pamela Sedgwick, 11 Nov. 1803, Sedgwick IV, Massachusetts Historical Society.
    [22]Catharine Maria Sedgwick to Theodore Sedgwick, 29 Dec. 1804, Sedgwick IV, Massachusetts Historical Society.
    [23]Theodore Sedgwick to Catharine Maria Sedgwick, 23 Apr. 1806, Sedgwick III, Massachusetts Historical Society.

creasingly popular children's miscellanies collected by Anna Bar-bauld and Arnaud Berquin.

Sedgwick, then, had little education in the "common sense," but there were "peculiar circumstances in my condition that in some degree supplied these great deficiencies." They were peculiar circumstances. Sedgwick was basically untutored and undirected, but as the result of living in a cultured household, "there was much chance seed dropped in the fresh furrow, and some of it was good seed." She was so bold to add, "some of it, I may say, fell on good ground." Sedgwick's metaphor highlights the paradoxical character of her education. Arbitrary, unstructured, and unpredictable as that education was, it had been obtained from a family that valued learning and considered the transmission of culture a responsibility, its possession a birthright.

Whether formal or informal, Sedgwick's education had not been designed to prepare her for a public career. Presuming that a daughter's existence would be centered in the home, elite families considered female education preparation for the role of wife and mother. Companion to husband and instructor to children, the educated woman was expected to dedicate herself to her family. This ideal of the wife and mother aside, the physical and emotional demands of domesticity made it difficult to engage in other pursuits. Ideology and circumstance, then, located a woman within the household and made the role she played there central to her identity. Any career beyond the home was decidedly unlikely. In contrast to nine out of ten women in the nineteenth century, Sedgwick remained unmarried. However, that unusual status had not made her eligible for a career. Instead, it was presumed that an unmarried woman would either remain with her parental family or attach herself to her siblings' families. Whatever the familial locus, the single woman's life was still defined in the context of domesticity.

Nonetheless, Sedgwick challenged prevailing experience and expectation. Her siblings, female and male, played significant albeit starkly different roles in their sister's decision to remain single. The experiences of Eliza and Frances were cautionary tales. Each of their marriages made tangible a gender hierarchy in which women were relatively powerless. The consequences for Frances were disastrous. Although Sedgwick described the marriage only sparingly in her autobiography, she captured its tone and temper in a single phrase—Frances "endured much heroically." In letters written to her other siblings, Sedgwick elaborated upon her sister's desperately unhappy union with Ebenezer Watson. The reason for Frances's distress was simple. As Sedgwick wrote to Eliza about Frances's husband, "Mr. Watson is *brutal* in his conduct to her and does and has for a long time rendered her miserable." With a demeanor that Sedgwick described as "oppressive," as "essentially diabolical," Ebenezer tyrannized Frances. Why, then, did Frances remain with her husband? That was also simple. Frances, as Sedgwick told Eliza in the same letter, "would leave him—but she cannot bear a separation from the children." This was no idle concern. Nineteenth-century legislation governing custody of children in the event of separation or divorce accorded the husband almost exclusive rights. That fact made Frances's situation "one of those hopeless miseries over which we must mourn without being able to remove it."[24] Throughout the crises that beset the marriage, Frances's brothers and sisters continued to provide sympathy and support. A resigned Frances remained in the marriage. Shortly before her elder sister's death in June 1842, Sedgwick wrote to a friend that Frances had been "through a life of vexing trials that would have cooled any love, exhausted any enthusiasm but hers."[25] The evidence suggests that was only a slight exaggeration.

In contrast to her sister Frances's experience, Eliza sustained a deeply caring marriage with Thaddeus Pomeroy. Nonetheless, this union as well entailed hardship. Eliza, Sedgwick recalled in the autobiography, had a "hard life of it—indifferent health and the painful drudgery of bearing and nurturing twelve children." Just as im-

[24]Catharine Maria Sedgwick to Eliza Pomeroy, 1 Dec. 1822, Sedgwick IV, Massachusetts Historical Society.
[25]Catharine Maria Sedgwick to Orville Dewey, 12 June 1842, in Dewey, ed., *Life and Letters of Catharine M. Sedgwick,* 281–282.

portant, nineteenth-century gender relations made the resolution of marital incompatibilities Eliza's responsibility. Thaddeus, as Sedgwick described him, "was a man after the old pattern—resolute, fearless, enduring, generous, with alterations of tenderness and austerity, of impulsiveness and rigidity." Unfortunately, some of these characteristics "were trying to [Eliza's] gentle disposition and unvarying and quiet devotion to duty." Four months before her sister's death in 1827, Sedgwick testified to Eliza's success in adapting to a marriage that resembled her parents'. Eliza, she declared in her journals, "can look back upon a life in which her duties have been well sustained." Her sister had been "an example of a Christian daughter and *sister*—wife and mother—friend and benefactor."[26] Sedgwick praised the obvious constancy. She commended the effort well performed. Only later in the autobiography did she remark upon the costs. Only then did she locate those costs in patriarchal gender relations.

While the experiences of Frances and Eliza contributed to Sedgwick's decision to remain unmarried, her brothers, all of whom welcomed her into their households, played the signal role. Offering care, affection, and companionship, Theodore, Harry, Robert, and Charles provided their sister with a familial base and made it possible for Sedgwick to create a marriage of circumstance. In a letter that she wrote when she was fifty-one, Sedgwick told her close friend Louisa Minot that "the affection that others give to husbands and children I have given to my brothers." She recognized that hers was an unusual situation. "Few," she noted, "can understand the dependence and intensity of my love for them."[27] Developed in childhood, that dependence and intensity increased in the wake of Theodore Sedgwick's death which occurred shortly after his youngest daughter's twenty-third birthday. Writing to her eldest brother ten days after their father had died on 24 January 1813, Sedgwick

[26]Journal of Catharine Maria Sedgwick, 10 June [1827], Catharine Maria Sedgwick Papers, Massachusetts Historical Society. See entry pp. 116–117.

[27]Catharine Maria Sedgwick to Louisa Minot, 5 Sept. 1841, Sedgwick IV, Massachusetts Historical Society.

told Theodore II that she longed to see him, longed to tell him that she felt "for all my brothers new sensations of love and dependence."[28]

In the decade following her father's death, Sedgwick's bond with two of her brothers increased in depth and strength. Each of these relationships had its particular character, each its particular expression of affection. Playfulness, remarkable wit, and shared sensibilities marked the intimacy Sedgwick shared with Harry. The attachment with Robert was charged with passion. Writing to him six months after their father's death, Sedgwick declared "I do love you, with a love surpassing at least the ordinary love of woman."[29] Six years later, she described him "as much a part of me as the lifeblood that flows through my heart."[30] Robert's declarations of affection were equally intense, his need for her equally strong. "My dear Kate," he told her on more than one occasion, "I know not how I could live without you."[31]

However, the trajectory of these relationships changed sharply in the 1820s. The years of mental illness that eventually cost Harry his life transformed all his relationships, not least the one that he had established with his sister Catharine. Beginning in 1827 and lasting until his death late in 1831, Sedgwick's journal is filled with expressions of overwhelming loss. In one of the many entries commenting on Harry's deteriorating condition, she lamented his "darkened mind," his "troubled spirit."[32] Still another entry described that once powerful mind as "a broken instrument." The spontaneity, the clarity, the discernment were gone forever. "Oh, it is too much," his

[28]Catharine Maria Sedgwick to Theodore Sedgwick II, 3 Feb. 1813, Sedgwick III, Massachusetts Historical Society.

[29]Catharine Maria Sedgwick to Robert Sedgwick, 2 July 1813, Catharine Maria Sedgwick Papers, Massachusetts Historical Society.

[30]Catharine Maria Sedgwick to Robert Sedgwick, 21 Nov. 1819, Catharine Maria Sedgwick Papers, Massachusetts Historical Society.

[31]Robert Sedgwick to Catharine Maria Sedgwick, 20 Nov. 1813, Sedgwick IV, Massachusetts Historical Society.

[32]Journal of Catharine Maria Sedgwick, 10 June [1827], Catharine Maria Sedgwick Papers, Massachusetts Historical Society. See entry p. 117.

sister cried out.[33] Sedgwick's desolation was sharpened by the felt reality of yet another loss that had occurred earlier in the decade. The reason was very different, although the impact seemed only slightly less. In December 1821, Robert had told his sister that he had decided to marry Elizabeth Ellery. "We cannot walk so close together as we have done," Sedgwick responded. That recognition devastated her: "No one can ever know all that I have, and must feel, because no one has ever felt the sheltering love, the tenderness, the friendship that left me nothing to desire."[34] Despite Robert's efforts to dissuade his sister, Sedgwick tried to lessen her dependence upon him. At the time of his marriage, Robert complained that she no longer spoke in "that language of the heart, by which you are accustomed so faithfully to interpret its emotions."[35] Nearly a year passed before Sedgwick felt sufficiently detached to acknowledge that her reticence had been motivated by the need to have his presence and profession of affection become "less necessary."[36] The connection, the sense of reciprocal commitment, established between sister and brother had become essential to Sedgwick's identity. Not surprisingly, then, the process of disengagement had been extremely painful.

Ultimately, Sedgwick achieved her objective of lessened dependence, although a deep attachment clearly persisted. After Harry's declining health required him and his wife Jane to leave New York City, Sedgwick spent her winters there with Robert and his family. She also traveled with them in Europe for fifteen months. But the intimacy, the mutual reliance sister and brother expressed in their letters prior to Robert's marriage, disappeared from their correspondence. Sedgwick herself alluded to the difference in an entry

---

[33]Journal of Catharine Maria Sedgwick, 31 Dec. 1828, Catharine Maria Sedgwick Papers. See entry p. 124.

[34]Catharine Maria Sedgwick to Robert Sedgwick, Dec. 1821, Catharine Maria Sedgwick Papers, Massachusetts Historical Society.

[35]Robert Sedgwick to Catharine Maria Sedgwick, 9 Aug. 1822, Sedgwick IV, Massachusetts Historical Society.

[36]Catharine Maria Sedgwick to Robert Sedgwick, 11 June 1823, Catharine Maria Sedgwick Papers, Massachusetts Historical Society.

dated 2 December 1837. The passage describes her relationships with members of her family, including Robert. But the sentences about him have been carefully inked out. In the margin alongside the passage, Sedgwick added the following on 24 July 1846, nearly five years after her brother's death: "Here I had written a lamentation over the transference of the first place in my dear brother Robert's heart. He had been father, lover as well as brother to me, and when in the inevitable concentration of a closer tie I felt an aching void, I expressed it as I should not."[37] Sedgwick immediately added "years passed on and I had proof that the love of our early years for a time without its usual demonstrations was there in that tenderest of hearts." That restored intimacy was Robert's gift to his sister in the final months before his death in September 1841.

The vacuum left by Harry and Robert was increasingly filled by Charles. The bond Sedgwick shared with the only brother younger than herself is documented in a correspondence that spanned nearly half a century. Theirs became a relationship in which reciprocity was perhaps the strongest hallmark. It seems appropriate that Sedgwick, an individual who had constituted herself in relation to others, should have experienced an exceptional mutuality in the sibling relationship that lasted the longest. Charles endeavored to "make my house, myself, my all as conducive to your happiness as it is possible it should be."[38] She emphasized that she had known "nothing of love—of memory—of hope—of which you are not an essential part."[39]

The losses and the shifting intensities notwithstanding, Sedgwick's deeply meaningful relationships with her brothers sustained her until Charles's death in 1856. Still, in entry upon entry in her journal, Sedgwick considered the consequences of her decision to

[37]Journal of Catharine Maria Sedgwick, 2 Dec. 1837, Catharine Maria Sedgwick Papers, Massachusetts Historical Society. See entry pp. 153–154.

[38]Charles Sedgwick to Catharine Maria Sedgwick, 2 Apr. 1848, Sedgwick IV, Massachusetts Historical Society.

[39]Catharine Maria Sedgwick to Charles Sedgwick, 2 Feb. 1829, Catharine Maria Sedgwick Papers, Massachusetts Historical Society.

remain single. As each of her brothers married, she became "first to none," as she phrased it in one of the early volumes of her journal.[40] Being "*second best*" was inevitably difficult.[41] It caused her the "keenest suffering." It surely constituted the "chief misery of single life."[42] And, as she recorded in her journal's last entry on 28 December 1854, she still felt "so acutely—so unworthily the inevitable change from the time when I was first in many hearts to being first in none."[43]

But if Sedgwick chose to highlight that cost in most of her entries, she also left meditations in her journal that located her choice in a larger and more balanced context. Yes, she had "suffered," she noted on 29 December 1834, the day after her forty-fifth birthday. But her life's more positive dimension was openly acknowledged—"for the most part I can look back upon a very happy life." Her literary career had brought her "far more of the world's respect than I ever expected." Her cherished friendships had continued undiminished through the years. The most important ties, the connections upon which she had constructed her core identity, had been more complicated. The marriages of her brothers had meant that "a portion of what was mine has been diverted into other channels." Acknowledging the pain that she still experienced, she said resignedly "my heart has ached and *does ache.*" Resignation was countered by a more resolute posture, however. She would not "repine," she would not be "exacting."[44] In another entry recorded two years later, Sedgwick meditated upon the alternative. The death of William Jarvis, one of her former suitors, provided the occasion. Whatever loneli-

[40]Journal of Catharine Maria Sedgwick, 18 May [1828], Catharine Maria Sedgwick Papers, Massachusetts Historical Society. See entry p. 122.

[41]Journal of Catharine Maria Sedgwick, 5 Aug. [1830], Catharine Maria Sedgwick Papers, Massachusetts Historical Society. See entry p. 127.

[42]Journal of Catharine Maria Sedgwick, 2 Dec. 1837, Catharine Maria Sedgwick Papers, Massachusetts Historical Society. See entry p. 153.

[43]Journal of Catharine Maria Sedgwick, 28 Dec. 1854, Catharine Maria Sedgwick Papers, Massachusetts Historical Society. See entry p. 158.

[44]Journal of Catharine Maria Sedgwick, 29 Dec. 1834, Catharine Maria Sedgwick Papers, Massachusetts Historical Society. See entry p. 148. She made another notable entry in this regard on 2 Dec. 1837. See entry pp. 152–154.

ness she had suffered, whatever pain her secondary status had entailed, Jarvis's death reminded Sedgwick of her conviction that a successful marriage required much more than the "liking" she had felt for the then "young man of five and twenty."[45]

It was not so much that Sedgwick regretted her decision to remain unmarried. Indeed, evidence indicates that she did not. And yet a relentlessly honest Sedgwick meditated upon the consequences of her choice throughout her life. That she vacillated, this time calmly accepting those consequences, that time lamenting them, suggests ambivalence. But Sedgwick was no simple woman, and neither was her ambivalence simple. Its complicated character she herself expressed concisely, profoundly, and perhaps unconsciously. "From my own experience," she said, "I would not advise any one to remain unmarried." For, she immediately added, "my experience has been a singularly happy one."[46]

Sedgwick's brothers were central to the choice she made about marriage. They were no less important in their sister's literary career. Strongly and consistently supportive, Theodore, Harry, Robert, and Charles served as her fraternal escorts. They encouraged the initially reluctant author, applauded the novels and stories, and negotiated with the publishers. In a letter written a decade before Sedgwick's appearance as a novelist, Harry displayed the enthusiasm with which he and his brothers fostered her career. Telling Sedgwick that he had agreed to edit Boston's *Weekly Messenger* every third week, he declared that he intended to print a portion of her recent letter—"a delightful scrap of yours on the sacred character of a *pastor.*" In his effort to bolster the confidence of female authors, he needed the "ammunition of a petticoated youth of high and early promise." None other than his sister would provide the necessary armament: "How confidently shall I claim for 'my fair countrywomen' the need of their genius; how triumphantly shall I

[45]Journal of Catharine Maria Sedgwick, 12 Oct. 1836, Catharine Maria Sedgwick Papers, Massachusetts Historical Society. See entry pp. 151–152.

[46]Journal of Catharine Maria Sedgwick, 18 May [1828], Catharine Maria Sedgwick Papers, Massachusetts Historical Society. See entry p. 123.

prove their precocity of intellect."[47] Harry's confidence in his sister was manifest. So too was his determination that she cultivate her talent. In asserting that the country must no longer neglect the genius of its women, he laid claim upon Sedgwick to display her own. Harry was also the first brother to persuade her to enlarge the form and scope of a religious tract she had begun after she left orthodox Congregationalism for Unitarianism. Theodore and Robert then joined forces with him, and they convinced their sister that the novel that emerged from the tract should be published.

Having read 130 pages of *A New England Tale* shortly after its publication in 1822, Theodore told Sedgwick that the novel "exceeds all my expectations, fond and flattering as they were." He had never doubted her abilities, but having seen them confirmed, his heart was filled with "pride and pleasure."[48] With the publication of Sedgwick's second novel two years later, Robert delighted in recounting to his sister that "wherever I go I receive compliments, felicitations, and even homage for the honor I have come to, by my relation to the author of *Redwood*."[49] Charles "rejoiced beyond all expression at the progress of the book" he was reading in manuscript.[50] The volume this time was *Hope Leslie*, Sedgwick's third novel, which appeared shortly after his heartening letter in the spring of 1827. Three years later, he told Sedgwick in mock horror that she must end her literary career or his "family will be ruined." Adults and children alike were locked away in their rooms absorbed with *Clarence*, Sedgwick's fourth novel.[51] So long as each was able, all of Sedgwick's brothers stayed the course, prompting, bolstering, and persuading their sister that her talent demanded literary expression. Dedicating

[47]Harry Sedgwick to Catharine Maria Sedgwick, 22 June 1812, Sedgwick IV, Massachusetts Historical Society.

[48]Theodore Sedgwick to Catharine Maria Sedgwick, 6 May 1822, in Dewey, ed., *Life and Letters of Catharine M. Sedgwick*, 152.

[49]Robert Sedgwick to Catharine Maria Sedgwick, 17 July 1824, Sedgwick IV, Massachusetts Historical Society.

[50]Charles Sedgwick to Catharine Maria Sedgwick, 28 Mar. 1827, Sedgwick IV, Massachusetts Historical Society.

[51]Charles Sedgwick to Catharine Maria Sedgwick, 21 May 1830, Sedgwick IV, Massachusetts Historical Society.

Clarence "To my Brothers—my best friends," Sedgwick acknowledged their signal importance to her career.

The elite standing of her family and the gender conventions of her century intersected in Sedgwick's career. The daughter of an influential Federalist, she nonetheless discarded the political convictions of her father and came to support the more egalitarian democracy he had found so threatening. However, two letters, both expressing Sedgwick's pleasure at favorable reactions to her fiction, highlight a lingering elitism that qualified her support for egalitarian democracy. "In this country," she succinctly informed her friend Louisa Minot, "we must do everything for the *majority*."[52] Elaborating upon her responsibilities to those who were numerically dominant, Sedgwick expressed her opinion to the clergyman William Ellery Channing that "there is an immense moral field opening demanding laborers." She, of course, defined herself as one of those laborers: "neither pride nor humility should withold us from the work to which we are clearly 'sent.'"[53]

In suggesting that elite status entailed particular responsibilities

[52]Catharine Maria Sedgwick to Louisa Minot, 26 Nov. 1836, Sedgwick IV, Massachusetts Historical Society.

[53]Catharine Maria Sedgwick to William Ellery Channing, 24 Aug. 1837, Catharine Maria Sedgwick Papers, Massachusetts Historical Society. The perspective of postrevolutionary writers is the subject of Emory Elliott, *Revolutionary Writers: Literature and Authority in the New Republic, 1725–1810* (New York, 1982). Positing a crisis of authority as the signal experience of these writers, Elliott suggests that they forged an identity more in keeping with the democratizing tendencies of the early republic. (Re)presenting themselves as disinterested and decidedly more humble, writers sought to instruct their readers without invoking the traditional authority with which earlier generations had invested themselves. The historical context for this development is provided in Joseph J. Ellis, *After the Revolution: Profiles of Early American Culture* (New York, 1979). Elliott and Ellis, each of whom considers only men, do not include gender as an analytical category. Gender is central to Cathy Davidson's highly suggestive study of these decades. See *Revolution and the Word: The Rise of the Novel in America* (New York, 1986), esp. 3–79. I have discussed gender and its relationship to literary authority in antebellum America in *Private Woman, Public Stage: Literary Domesticity in Nineteenth-Century America* (New York, 1984), esp. 111–214. Michael Warner analyzes the implications of transformations in print discourse and reading that took place in 18th-century America. Richard Brown's study of the same phenomenon extends the analysis into the 19th century. See Warner, *The Letters of the Republic: Publication and the Public Sphere in Eighteenth-Century America* (Cambridge, Mass., 1990); Brown, *Knowledge Is Power: The Diffusion of Information in Early America, 1700-1865* (New York, 1989).

to the larger society, Sedgwick had to address a basic question: was there any role for individuals of privilege in an increasingly democratic antebellum America? Despite the claims that resonated through these decades, America's democracy remained decidedly limited—barriers to participation either as voters or as jurors remained in force for African-American men and for women of all races. Universal suffrage for white men had made them equal at the polls. In defining the obligations as cultural rather than political, Sedgwick envisioned an elite that might yet be critical to the success of a society that defined itself as democratic. Those who could no longer expect to dominate at the polls could retain power and authority in the domain of culture. And there they could continue to "do everything for the *majority*." But was it possible for a *woman* to invest herself with the obligations she had accorded an elite? Entitled by her family's status to enrich herself intellectually and culturally, Sedgwick took a further step and defined herself as a participant in the construction of culture. Had she clung to the political model of elite dominance, she, like all women regardless of status, would have been excluded from participation in the national project. In combining the increasingly popular idea that women should be moral guardians with the long-standing conviction that culture should be informed by moral as well as aesthetic purpose, Sedgwick was able to circumvent barriers based on gender and transform the legacy that Theodore Sedgwick had intended only for his sons. She could now see herself as Channing's equal and insist that they both dedicate themselves to the "work to which we are clearly 'sent.'"[54]

[54]In a study published nearly 60 years ago, William Charvat identified the linkage between the aesthetic and the moral made by antebellum Americans in defining the purpose of culture. The importance that Unitarian leaders such as William Ellery Channing attached to this linkage has been explored by Daniel Walker Howe. Lawrence Buell has been done the same for New England's writers more generally. The related linkage between the moral and the feminine has received consideration from scholars studying women and antebellum reform. Lori Ginzberg's recent study of elite women's participation in organized benevolence is particularly insightful in this regard. Perhaps most notably, she has highlighted a strategy justifying female participation that was remarkably similar to Sedgwick's. See Charvat, *The Origins of American Critical Thought, 1810-1835* (Philadelphia, 1936); Howe, *The Unitarian Conscience: Harvard*

Simultaneously, however, Sedgwick's elite standing generated ambivalence about the prominence that followed from the exercise of power and authority. Ranked with the early nineteenth century's most prominent writers, Sedgwick acknowledged the pleasure of distinction. Yes, she conceded in a journal entry recorded shortly after the publication of *Hope Leslie*, she delighted in being one of antebellum America's most notable literary figures, in "being able to command a high station wherever I go." But that distinction also entailed what her brother Charles aptly termed "Lafayettism," a condition in which the subject became the possession of her public. Having been "introduced to multitudes at [Saratoga] Springs who paid this compliment to what they deemed my literary success," Sedgwick found the experience distasteful. She had "to fritter away in general courtesies time and thought and feeling." It was a "disadvantage" that she felt deeply. That Sedgwick sought the betterment of those same multitudes was obvious. That she sought influence as a cultural arbiter was equally so. Nonetheless, she still longed for the deference that would have insulated her from the claims an increasingly aggressive public made upon its famous. She still longed to be aloof.[55]

The claims that Sedgwick made on behalf of elite women privi-

---

Moral Philosophy, 1805–1861 (Cambridge, Mass., 1970); Buell, *New England Literary Culture: From Revolution Through Renaissance* (Cambridge, 1986); Ginzberg, *Women and the Work of Benevolence: Morality, Politics and Class in the Nineteenth-Century United States* (New Haven, 1990).

[55]Michael T. Gilmore's analysis of Emerson, Hawthorne, Thoreau, and Melville has identified a similar response to the larger and less elite public in antebellum America. Deeply ambivalent in their reaction to popularity, they simultaneously sought to cultivate that public and to resist its claims. Stephen Railton has explored the rhetorical responses that these writers inscribed in their texts. He has also expanded the exploration to include Poe and Stowe. Noting the same increase in the number of Americans that constituted the public, Donald M. Scott has examined the changing relationship between knowledge and the marketplace. No longer the possession of an elite, knowledge itself had become a commodity available for purchase by any literate American. Stow Persons's insightful study explores the implications of all these changes. See Gilmore, *American Romanticism and the Marketplace* (Chicago, 1985), esp. 1–17; Railton, *Authorship and Audience: Literary Performance in the American Renaissance* (Princeton, 1991); Scott, "Knowledge and the Marketplace," in James Gilbert, Amy Gilman, Donald M. Scott, and Joan W. Scott, eds., *The Mythmaking Frame of Mind: Social Imagination*

leged conduct that was simultaneously disinterested and deeply informed with moral purpose. The degree to which Sedgwick identified with these attributes can be seen in the reflections on literary
women that are scattered through her autobiography and journal.
Sometimes the subject she chose was herself. Shortly after the publication of *Hope Leslie*, Sedgwick recorded a meditation on the meaning of fame. Noting in her journal that "my fond friends expect a
great accession of fame to me," she asked herself that spring of 1827,
"fame—what is it?" The praise that had marked the publication of
her novel was dismissed as nothing more than the transient "breath
of man." Fame was welcomed only if it was endowed with purpose,
only if her achievements "produced some good feeling."[56] Almost
as frequently, the subject was other women who had broken ground
as participants in the construction of culture. Sedgwick's meditations in this regard appeared almost as reflections in a mirror. In
contemplating other literary women, this participant in her nation's
intellectual and cultural enterprise contemplated herself. Nonetheless, Sedgwick had to look abroad for counterparts during the for-
mative decades of her career. In contrast to the Englishwomen with
whom she compared herself, she stood nearly alone as a prominent
American writer who happened to be a woman.

After Sedgwick had met the English writer Harriet Martineau
during the latter's visit to the United States in the early 1830s, she
devoted one of her journal's longer entries to her. Considering
Sedgwick's earlier reservations about the political economist, the
impression made by Martineau in person was all the more telling.
Initially, Sedgwick had thought that the pursuit of such a masculine
enterprise "was not the loveliest manifestation of woman." But
Martineau, whom Sedgwick calls "extraordinary," had allayed this
concern almost immediately. She had been "so modest, gentle, and
kind." She had exhibited such a venerable combination of "genius

---

and American Culture (Belmont, Calif., 1992), 99–112; Persons, *The Decline of American
Gentility* (New York, 1973).

[56]Journal of Catharine Maria Sedgwick, 10 June 1827, Catharine Maria Sedgwick
Papers, Massachusetts Historical Society. See entry p. 118.

and virtue."[57] That Sedgwick considered virtue more important became obvious in a second entry comparing Martineau to Anna Barbauld, Maria Edgeworth, Anna Jameson, and Felicia Hemans, all of
whom had been successful in their literary careers. None, however,
had achieved Martineau's prominence. Sedgwick asked herself why.
Certainly, the others had "shown as powerful a genius as hers." Indeed, Sedgwick considered some of them superior in this regard.
Nonetheless, Martineau had distinguished herself in her singular
commitment of "God's good gifts to the use of his creatures." She
had made the common good the sine qua non of her career. Martineau had also been decidedly inclusive in her definition of those
creatures. Leaving to others "the intellectual amusement or advancement of the gifted and educated," Martineau had focused
upon the multitudes. That egalitarianism had made "us all cry Hail
thou favored among women!"[58]

The two entries revealed at least as much about Sedgwick as
about Martineau, their putative subject. Perhaps most notably, they
demonstrated the remarkable agility with which Sedgwick was able
to negotiate antebellum America's gender conventions. Erasing her
initial suspicion that political economy was most properly a masculine enterprise, Sedgwick made its practitioner the embodiment of
femininity. Still more tellingly, she complicated the common premise that men alone were lords of creation, a popular phrase that
signaled the gender conventions limiting participation in the construction of culture. In ascribing creativity, or "genius," to Martineau, Barbauld, Edgeworth, Jameson, and Hemans, Sedgwick
openly contradicted those who located generative power exclusively
in the masculine. Yet for all the boldness of her challenge, the burden of Sedgwick's commentary was more in keeping with than set
against prevailing gender conventions. Most strikingly, Sedgwick
made "virtue," a concept increasingly associated with women, an

---

[57]Journal of Catharine Maria Sedgwick, 8 Oct. [1834], Catharine Maria Sedgwick
Papers, Massachusetts Historical Society. See entry pp. 144–146.

[58]Journal of Catharine Maria Sedgwick, 9 Aug. 1835, Catharine Maria Sedgwick Papers, Massachusetts Historical Society. See entry pp. 148–149.

equally important qualification for participation in the construction of culture. Although the precise meaning of virtue was contested among antebellum Americans, all generally agreed that dedication to the common good was central to its definition and that women's potential for such dedication exceeded men's. Negotiating the highly charged gender conventions and designing a readily identifiable persona from those conventions, Sedgwick had made culture Martineau's domain. Simultaneously, she had done the same for herself.

The aesthetic and moral purpose, the disinterested commitment, the identification of women with a newly conceptualized virtue, in short, the strategies Sedgwick employed in positioning herself as a writer all figured in the pages of her fiction. In the original preface to *A New England Tale,* she described the novel as an "effort to add something to the scanty stock of native American literature."[59] That it did. The novel offered its readers contemporary New England in scenery and characters, including the Yankee peddler, whom Sedgwick introduced to American literature. In the preface to the second edition issued three months after the novel's publication, the author stressed that *A New England Tale* was also informed by a moral purpose. The novel, she told readers, "was written under a sincere conviction of its beneficial tendency."[60] Sedgwick was specifically concerned that her motives might be misconstrued by those who aligned themselves with the prevailing Calvinism. In a letter written jointly with Harry, she told Theodore that "there is no condemnation of doctrines, but only of their abuse in individuals."[61] The statement was nominally correct. Doctrinal issues are left aside in the novel, but Sedgwick's sympathies are barely disguised. Her staunchest Calvinist is portrayed as a hypocrite and her behavior juxtaposed against the exemplary conduct of those who profess a

---

[59]Catharine Maria Sedgwick, *A New England Tale: or; Sketches of New England Character and Manners* (New York, 1852/1822), 9.

[60]Sedgwick, *New England Tale*, 11.

[61]Catharine Maria Sedgwick and Harry Sedgwick to Theodore Sedgwick, [29 Mar. 1822], Sedgwick II, Massachusetts Historical Society.

more humane Christianity. Almost certainly, the experience of Sedgwick's sisters influenced the fledgling novelist's portrayal of Calvinism. In her autobiography, Sedgwick recalled that both Eliza and Frances had "suffered from the horrors of Calvinism." The impact on Eliza had been particularly destructive—she had believed "its monstrous doctrines, and they [had] made her gloomy." Once she had been freed from the insidious implications of this doctrinal system, Eliza had experienced an indescribable happiness of "redemption from the cruel doctrines of Geneva." In Sedgwick's juxtaposition of characters, both the miseries of Calvinism and the elation of release from its doctrines were readily apparent.

The novel's primary significance derives nonetheless from Sedgwick's presentation of the heroine, Jane Elton. Sympathy, integrity, and fortitude are combined in Jane with a "rare habit of putting *self* aside." Rare or not, the selflessness exhibited by Jane was a presumed attribute in nineteenth-century women. Sedgwick also invests her heroine with notable strength. Left "poor, helpless, and friendless" after the death of her parents, Jane refuses to submit to seemingly endless adversities and emerges from her trials resiliant, secure, and independent. She emerges as well with her humanitarian impulses intact.[62] Sedgwick's second novel, *Redwood*, deals with the experiences of another orphaned heroine whose disinterested conduct parallels her earlier counterpart.

In the preface to her third novel, published in 1827, Sedgwick informed her readers that she had taken a different approach. Noting that she had located *Hope Leslie* in seventeenth-century New England, she told them that her historical novel had been designed as a means by which others might be prompted "to investigate the early history of their native land."[63] She returned to the present in her fourth novel, *Clarence: A Tale of Our Own Times*. Significantly, *Clarence* took exception to those times. Indeed, the novel is a damn-

[62]Sedgwick, *New England Tale*, 165, 21.

[63]Catharine Maria Sedgwick, *Hope Leslie: or, Early Times in Massachusetts* (New Brunswick, 1987), 2. Originally published in 1827, this novel is now available as part of the American Women Writers Series published by Rutgers University Press.

ing commentary on an antebellum America that increasingly made wealth the sole determinant of status. Principled and cultured characters are juxtaposed against unscrupulous and vulgar representatives of fashionable society. Satire marks the pages in which the fashionable are mocked and ostentation ridiculed. Sedgwick's primary conviction was unmistakable—only talent and moral integrity should determine rank, only those exhibiting both characteristics deserve emulation. Sedgwick changed course yet again in *The Linwoods; or "Sixty Years Since" in America*, a second historical novel which she published in 1835. Set in Revolutionary New York and complete with prominent figures including George Washington, the novel celebrates the colonists' struggle for independence. In contrast to her criticism of the Puritans in *Hope Leslie*, Sedgwick chose to commend this earlier generation because she sought to promote her readers' gratitude to their ancestors, "a sentiment that will tend to increase their fidelity to the free institutions transmitted to them."[64] Spurred by the enormous popularity of Sir Walter Scott, Sedgwick sought to recover her nation's past, to kindle interest in its early inhabitants, and to foster a cultural identity other than that derived from the former mother country. The highly favorable response to both of Sedgwick's historical novels suggests that she achieved these objectives.

When Sedgwick published her last novel in 1857, twenty-two years had elapsed since *The Linwoods* had appeared. Her topic was appropriate, her title equally so—*Married or Single?* addresses the question Sedgwick posed for herself and considered throughout her journal. In the novel, Sedgwick acknowledged marriage as "the central point, whence all the relations of life radiate, and the source of all political and social virtue."[65] But she also ridiculed the idea "that matrimony is essential to the feebler sex—that a woman's single life must be useless or undignified—that she is but an adjunct of man." Instead, she said, "we believe she has an independent power to

---

[64] *The Linwoods; or, Sixty Years Since in America*, 2 vols. (New York, 1835), 1:xii.
[65] Catharine Maria Sedgwick, *Married or Single?*, 2 vols. (New York, 1857), 2:81.

shape her own course, and to force her separate sovereign way."[66] But to do what? Not surprisingly, the single woman who had made her own way derived satisfaction from the same sources that had sustained Sedgwick herself. It was the reciprocal relationships forged as sister, friend, benefactor that gave an unmarried woman's life meaning. These convictions served as a fitting testimony for the woman who had defined herself in relation to others, who had told William Minot that she had "had my home in so many houses and so many hearts."

The same year that Sedgwick presented *The Linwoods* to an admiring public, she published a narrative that indicated a departure in form if not in substance from her earlier literary endeavors. Fellow Unitarian Henry Ware, Jr., had provided the catalyst. Writing to Sedgwick in January 1834, he had invited her to contribute to a series of volumes "offering to the public an exhibition of the practical character and influences of Christianity." The form he suggested differed from any that Sedgwick had attempted—a narrative that stood "between a formal tale and a common tract."[67] Published in 1835, *Home: Scenes and Character Illustrating Christian Truth* did exactly that. During the latter part of the 1830s, three similar volumes appeared, all of which were directed toward the inculcation of proper behavior. *Poor Rich Man and Rich Poor Man* (1836) insisted that genuine riches came from "the voluntary exercise of those virtues that produce an interchange of benevolent offices."[68] *Live and Let Live* (1837) and *Means and Ends* (1839), both of which were dedicated to "My Young Countrywomen," lauded domesticity as a worthy locus for a woman's identity and stressed preparation for her marital role. Simultaneously, Sedgwick continued to publish a steady stream of tales and sketches in annuals and leading periodicals, including *Godey's*, *Graham's*, and *Harper's*. (Twenty-one selec-

---

[66]Sedgwick, *Married or Single?*, 1:vi.

[67]Henry Ware, Jr., to Catharine Maria Sedgwick, 31 Jan. 1834, in Dewey, ed., *Life and Letters of Catharine M. Sedgwick*, 239.

[68]Catharine Maria Sedgwick, *The Poor Rich Man, and the Rich Poor Man* (New York, 1837), 39.

tions from nearly a hundred of these tales and sketches appeared in two volumes, in 1835 and 1844). Dominated by the same subjects explored in the novels, they themselves constitute an impressive body of fiction. Tangled romances, satires denigrating fashionable society, tributes to contented spinsters, portraits of New England villages, chronicles of ideal marriages, all are handled with stylistic clarity, subtle wit, and unusual grace.

In a letter that is emblematic of the devotion Sedgwick inspired in virtually everyone with whom she shared herself, the youngest of her siblings told her that she had been the recipient of many gifts. By far the one for which she should be most grateful was the most obvious—"the power of your sympathy," as Charles described his sister's deep and sustaining identification with others.[69] The designation was appropriate for both Sedgwick the person and the gender conventions of her century. In her autobiography, in her journal, in her fiction, in short, in all of her writings, she had insisted upon the signal importance of connection in her relations with others. Indeed, she had presented herself as entirely interwoven with others. Nineteenth-century gender conventions which located in women a special capacity for selflessness also privileged connection as feminine. Yet Charles neglected to mention the equal significance that Sedgwick attached to the freedom to choose for oneself. Based on the premise that women had a claim on individual fulfillment, choice had enormous implications for women in a century in which they were expected to subordinate themselves to the needs and desires of men. In her writings and in the most important decisions taken in her life, Sedgwick made those implications tangible. The issues she selected covered a broad spectrum—decisions regarding religious affiliation, vocational commitment, and marital identity were included in her domain. The gender conventions of her century constructed connection and choice almost as a binary opposition. Inflected as feminine and masculine, choice appeared possible

---

[69]Charles Sedgwick to Catharine Maria Sedgwick, [June 1837], Sedgwick IV, Massachusetts Historical Society.

only for men. But Sedgwick deconstructed this opposition and made connection and choice complementary imperatives for both sexes. Insisting that women should freely and fully choose a life for themselves, she suggested that only then could they just as freely and fully practice connection. No longer marked as exclusively feminine, connection could be a mutual practice for women and men. In this as in so much else, she displayed the insight, or as Charles phrased it, the power of her sympathy, that made her autobiography and her journal compelling.

Autobiography

May 5, 1853

My dear little Alice,

[It is now] about two years since your father wrote me an eloquent note persuading me to write for you some memories of my life, and what I knew of your forbears and mine. If you live to be an old woman, as I now am, you may like to rake in the ashes of the past, and if, perchance, you find some fire still smouldering there, you may feel a glow from it. It is not till we get deep into age that we feel by how slight a tenure we hold on to the memories of those that come after us, and not till then that we are conscious of an earnest desire to brighten the links of the chain that binds us to those who have gone before, and to keep it fast and strong.

The first of our Sedgwick ancestors of whom I have any tradition was Robert Sedgwick, who was sent by Oliver Cromwell as governor or commissioner (I am not sure by which title) to the island of Jamaica.[1] As I am a full believer in the transmission of qualities peculiar to a race, it pleases me to recognize in "the governor," as we have always called him, a Puritan and an Independent, for to none other would Cromwell have given a trust so important. A love of freedom, a habit of doing their own thinking, has characterized our clan. Its men have not been trammeled by old usages, but for the most part have stood on those elevations that first catch the light and command a wide horizon. (There, my dear! I have not got over the second page without betraying my point of family pride and family weakness!) Truly I think it a great honor that the head of our house took office from that great man who achieved his own greatness, and not from the King Charleses who were born to it, and lost it by their own unworthiness.

Of my mother's progenitors I only know that, according to the

---

[1]Colonist, soldier, and merchant, Robert Sedgwick (c. 1613–1656) settled in New England in 1636. During the next two decades, he served as captain for Charlestown, Massachusetts, helped to organize the military company for the colony, and served as a legislator in the General Court. Sedgwick's information about his service in the West Indies was faulty, however. Neither commissioner nor governor, he did head a military expedition that Oliver Cromwell dispatched to fortify the occupation after the English had seized the Island of Jamaica from the Spanish. He died there in 1656.

general New England foundation, *three* brothers—Englishmen—
came together to the New World; that they were men of character
and estate; and that from one of them my mother descended. The
riches went, not in our channel, but to that branch from which
your kind and dear friends Mrs. Parkman and cousin Lizzie Dwight
came. Riches and our name have no affinities, my dear! The wise
man's prayer has been granted to us; we have enjoyed fully the advantage and felicity of being neither rich nor poor! My maternal
grandfather [Joseph Dwight] was a brigadier colonel in the war in
the French Provinces in 1745. The family tradition goes that he was
at the taking of Cape Breton, and that he served with honor.[2] You
see his picture at "Father Charles's,"[3] a handsome, hale man, with
ruddy cheeks and most delicately beautiful hands, rather studiously
displayed. I am afraid he had a weakness on that point; or perhaps
he showed them to prove to his descendants that he had kept "clean
hands," a commendable virtue, physically or morally speaking. He
was one of the gentlemen par excellence of his time, who maintained the highest associations of the province. I have heard an old
Irish servant of his, who maintained a feudal reverence for him, and
who used to visit this portrait in the best parlor of our old Stockbridge home, say often, as he stood before it with the tears rolling
off his cheeks, "Oh, if you could have seen him with his rigimintals,
he would have scared you!"[4]

[2]Located on Cape Breton Island at the entrance to the St. Lawrence River, the heavily
fortified Louisbourg was besieged by a land force of New Englanders supported by the
Royal Navy. The French, who capitulated before the combined operation, recovered
the colony in 1748, the year in which the Treaty of Aix-la-Chapelle ended King
George's War.

[3]Charles Sedgwick, Catharine's brother and Alice's grandfather.

[4]Sedgwick's maternal grandfather, Joseph Dwight (1703–1765), was the son of Henry
and Lydia Hawley Dwight, both of whom came from prominent families in the Connecticut River Valley. After graduation from Harvard College, Dwight achieved similar
prominence as a lawyer and land speculator in the Valley. His marriage to Abigail Williams Sergeant brought him to Stockbridge, Massachusetts, where he became resident
trustee of the Indian school. His wife, Abigail, headed the female counterpart. Together
they profited handsomely from the funds the government provided the schools. Their
behavior also brought them into conflict with Jonathan Edwards, then the minister for
both the English and Housatonic residents of Stockbridge. Although Edwards eventu-

My grandmother was a widow of Mr. Sergeant, missionary from a Scotch society to the Indians, when my grandfather married her. Her maiden name was Williams. She was the sister of the founder of Williams College, and a woman much celebrated in her day for her intelligence and character.[5] I have not, like you, my dear Alice, ever enjoyed the pleasure of this relation, which extends our being by one generation, and gives us the twilight as well as the dawn. My father's mother died long before I was born; my mother's mother, I think, about eighteen months after. I have always heard her spoken of as a remarkable woman in her time, but my most vivid impression of her is from the record of Mrs. Quincy, who, when she was [Eliza] Susan Morton and a young girl, had an enthusiastic love for her mother's old friend, "Madam Dwight," and twice made a pilgrimage to Stockbridge to see her. I shall copy her account for your benefit. . . .[6]

> Madam Dwight of Stockbridge came to visit us in 1786. The daughter of Colonel Williams, of Williamstown, she married Mr. Sergeant, of Stockbridge, who died in early life, leaving two sons; and his widow

---

ally prevailed, the social and economic standing that Joseph and Abigail Dwight had achieved remained secure.

[5] The daughter of Ephraim and Elizabeth Jackson Williams, Abigail Williams Sergeant Dwight (1721–1791) was actually the half sister of Ephraim Williams, the founder of Williams College. She married John Sergeant, a missionary who headed an Indian school in Stockbridge, Massachusetts, in 1739. They had two sons and a daughter before Sergeant's death in 1749. Their third child, John Sergeant, also became a missionary to Stockbridge's Indians after they had been removed to the state of New York. Her second husband, Joseph Dwight, had an entirely secular interest in Stockbridge's Indians. He became Abigail's partner in the management of the Indian schools in Stockbridge and, as noted in the previous citation, made substantial money from their enterprise. They had two children, Henry and Pamela.

[6] The daughter of John and Maria Morton, Eliza Susan Morton Quincy (c. 1774–1850) was introduced to Abigail Dwight during the latter's visit with her family in New York City. In 1794, Morton married Josiah Quincy, later the mayor of Boston and president of Harvard. Quincy's description of Abigail Dwight can be found in her *Memoir of the Life of Eliza S. M. Quincy* (Boston, 1861), 47–50. After noting that she would copy Quincy's recollection of Dwight, Sedgwick left the next six pages blank. These pages were clearly set aside for the description that Quincy published in her memoir. In the *Life and Letters of Catharine M. Sedgwick*, Mary E. Dewey copied Quincy's description almost verbatim. Her version has been used here in place of a similar transcribed text on pp. 8–10 of the manuscript.

became the wife of Colonel Dwight, one of the leading men of Massachusetts in his day. Their children were Henry Dwight, and Pamela, afterward Mrs. Theodore Sedgwick. Madam Dwight was again left a widow, and in 1786 was upward of sixty years of age, tall and erect, dignified, precise in manner, yet benevolent and pleasing. Her dress, of rich silk, a high-crowned cap, with plaited border, and a watch, then so seldom worn as to be a distinction, all marked the gentlewoman, and inspired respect. She was a new study to me, and realized my ideas of Mrs. Shirley in "Sir Charles Grandison," and other characters I had read of in works of fiction.[7] When she returned home she asked me to accompany her, and, to my great joy, her request was complied with. We went up the Hudson in a sloop, in which we were the only passengers.

We staid at Kinderhook till the wagon came for us from Stockbridge. I was seated by Madam Dwight, and we were driven by her grandson, a son of Dr. Sergeant. The distance was thirty or forty miles—a day's journey. It was twilight when we reached Stockbridge. The first thing that attracted my attention was a fish for a vane, on the steeple of the church. I said to Madam Dwight, "How could they put up a poor fish, so much out of its own element? It ought at least to have been a flying fish." She seemed much diverted at my remark, and repeated it to her friends, confessing that she had never thought of this absurdity herself, or heard it observed by others. Dr. Sergeant, Madam Dwight's son by her first marriage, resided in her mansion-house, where she retained the best parlor and chamber for her own use. He was an excellent man, and the most distinguished physician in that part of the country. We were joyfully received by him and his family. As I was fatigued, Madam Dwight took me to her room, and again expressed her pleasure at having me with her. I can never forget her affection and kindness. Her precepts and example made an indelible impression in favor of virtue and true piety. Her temper and character formed a living mirror, which reflected an image of such loveliness that my heart was truly bound to her. She made me her companion, read to me, and talked to me with the confidence of a friend.

When, on the morning after our arrival, the window-shutters were opened, the Valley of the Housatonic, softened by wreaths of vapor rising over the mountains under the beams of the rising sun,

---

[7]The English baronet Sir Charles Grandison is the hero of Samuel Richardson's novel of the same name. The venerable widow Henrietta Shirley serves as a surrogate mother for the orphaned heroine Harriet Byron.

seemed to my enchanted vision like fairy-land. I exclaimed, "O, Madam Dwight ! it looks like the Happy Valley of Abyssinia. There is the river, and there are the mountains on every side. Why did you never tell me of this beautiful view?" My friend seemed surprised at my enthusiasm. Long familiar with the scene, she hardly realized its beauty. I became attached to her grandchildren, and passed several months in Stockbridge. Her daughter, Mrs. [Pamela Dwight] Sedgwick, lived upon "the Plain," as it was called, in distinction to "the Hill," where Dr. Sergeant resided.

When I was recalled home, I parted from Madam Dwight with great reluctance, and she expressed equal sensibility. She endeavored to comfort me by saying that she would visit New York the next spring, and that I should return with her. But she was prevented from executing this intention; and when I revisited Stockbridge in 1792, my friend was no more.

My mother and Henry Dwight, who occupied the house at the west end of "the Plain," were the only children of the marriage of my grandmother with Colonel Dwight. They had both been previously married. My grandmother had three children by the first marriage—Erastus, John, and Electa [Sergeant]. Erastus was our "Uncle Doctor," a distinguished physician in Berkshire for nearly fifty years. He was a mild, faithful man, and patient as the best of Christians are with the severest domestic afflictions. John succeeded his father as missionary to the Indians. I believe he worked faithfully in the field, but I never could hear that the poor man reaped any harvest. His Indians had lost the masculine savage quality, the wild flavor, and had imbibed the dreg-vices of civilization, without in the least profiting by its advantages. He was the "Uncle John" Sergeant of my childhood, not the "*Uncle John*" I shall hereafter tell you. Electa became "Aunt Hopkins," and was the ancestor of the present President and Professor of Williams College. The President is one of our best moral writers.

There was a traditionary story of my mother's childhood which used to affect my imagination, for in my youth, dear Alice, the dark shadows of the Indians had hardly passed off our valleys, and tales about them made the stock terrors of our nurseries. The Indians of New England were at that time—about 1750—friendly to the white people, but the Mohawks were a terror to the whites, and to their red friends. My mother was about two years old when my grandmother was on a visit with her to her son Erastus (Dr. Sergeant) in Stockbridge. The servant-men only were at home—a black man and Lynch, the Irish servant whom I have already mentioned. There was an alarm—the hideous cry, "The Indians are coming!" There were no horses in the stable, and the women decided at once to set off on foot. My grandmother gave her little girl Pamela (my mother) to the black servant, and dispatched him. Lynch followed soon after, and, descending the hill, heard a faint cry from a thick copse by the roadside. The cry came from the poor little girl, whom the terrified man had relieved himself of as soon as out of sight. Lynch took her up and carried her to a place of safety. The Indians did not come, but Lynch ever after looked upon himself as a hero in our family annals, and, in truth, pretty much as its founder. Poor old man! It was a proud day for him when "the Judge" (my dear father) and all "the family" went in "the old coachee" to dine with him. His tremulous voice and shaking hands were almost firm again as he stood at his door in *Larrywaug* to welcome us. His name was Lawrence, and "waug" is Indian for a cluster of houses, so the little hamlet at the west end of Stockbridge was named for him. I do not know if it has yet lost the designation.

Through all my childhood, Larry Lynch was the only Irish inhabitant of Stockbridge! I do not believe there were then half a dozen in the county! I think their influx did not begin before 1830—and now there are two thronged churches in Berkshire, and occasional mass in all the villages where they swarm. What would dear old Dr. West, our sixty years Defender of the Puritan Faith (the Doric pillar of Hopkinsianism), what would he say to these multitudinous children of Antichrist![8] One of the oldest members of his Church, Mrs.

[8]Stephen West (1735–1819) succeeded Jonathan Edwards as Stockbridge's minister in 1758. A graduate of Yale College, West was deeply influenced by the noted Calvinist Samuel Hopkins. West's ministry, which brought an undeviating message of predestination and election to his parishioners for nearly six decades, was obviously opposed to the doctrines of Roman Catholicism. Sedgwick describes the minister and his theological position on pp. 95–99.

Ingersoll, the deacon's wife, after the departure of her meek help-mate (he was the weaker vessel), rented the deacon's old hat-shop—he was hat manufacturer to the village—to Billy Brogan. It was a little, one-story, unpainted building, in the same enclosure with her house. None but an Irish family would have gathered there. When the Irish became numerous enough, mass was to be celebrated in the village, and Billy Brogan's habitation was selected as the largest domicile among them, and therefore fittest for the holy purpose. Nothing could exceed the indignation of the deacon's widow—a Yankee Mause—nor the energy of her invectives, necessarily re-strained within the decencies of Puritan objurgation.[9] To have mass on her premises—a Catholic priest within her gates—"mass in the deacon's shop! the shop turned into a *Cathedral!* No, she had rather burn it!"

The result of this new experiment in the world of a distinct race, with marked characteristics and a religion of their own, living among us with the full benefit of equal rights and privileges, you, my dear Alice, may live to see. But, as ignorance cannot compete with knowledge, nor get the mastery of it till there is an immense odds of brute force, as a despotic religion has neither sanction nor security in the midst of free institutions, I trust, my dear child, that the Irish, by the infusion of an element of warmth and generosity into our national character, will have done us more good than evil. I am inclined to think they have already done this for us. I have so lively a recollection of the time when we were in the transitive state—when the old well-trained slaves had disappeared—when the few black servants to be hired were shiftless, lazy, and unfaithful, and our own people scarcely to be obtained, and, if obtained, they came "to accomodate you," and stayed only till they could accomo-date themselves better, that I felt grateful for Irish *servants*, with all their Celtic infirmities on their heads—their half savage ways—their blunders—their imaginativeness—indefiniteness—

[9]Mause Headrigg, a character in Walter Scott's *Old Mortality*, was a highly vocal supporter of the Covenantors in their revolt against the English crown. The outspoken self-righteousness of Mrs. Ingersoll made her a Yankee version in Sedgwick's eyes.

and *curve-lines* every way. They desire employment—they are willing servants—they are sympathetic and progressive—and I have at this moment, June 1853, a girl in my service, Margaret Pollock, a pearl of great price. She is a Protestant, to be sure, but she was born and bred in Ireland, and I would not exchange her for all the service I could distill in Yankeedom.

I have sore recollections of the time when I rode the country round to get, for love *and* money, girls to do the family work. Unwilling [they were] to come and incompetent when they came. My father's house was one of the few where the domestics were restricted to the kitchen table. "Oh," said a woman to me, whose daughter I was begging for, "now Catha*rine*, we are all made out of the same clay, we have got one Maker and one Judge, and we've got to lay down in the grave side by side. Why can't you sit down to the table together?" We were vexed and fretted, and thought the people presuming, impertinent, and stupid; but stupid they were not, and we were not philosophers. They used their power; they had something better before them than domestic subordination and household service. *Their* time had come, their harness was thrown off, fresh pastures were before them. They did not, perhaps, use their freedom gracefully, but they enjoyed it, and it was theirs. The West and the factories have absorbed all this population, and Providence has sent the starving hewers of wood and drawers of water from other lands to us to be taught in our kitchens, and to [be] borne on by the mighty wave of progress that is steadily tending onward and upward here. It is not left to our choice. Providence makes of our homes Irish school-houses! of our mother and daughters involuntary missionaries.

Thus, if you will but observe it, dear Alice, you will see that God works more effectively than man, in a wider field, and with greater means. He sets the sun in the sky, and it lights the world; we are proud of the gaslights that dispel the darkness of a city, just enabling us to know a friend from a stranger. God sends rain over our wide tracts of land, refreshing harvest fields, ripening the fruits of the earth, nourishing our gardens, and filling *rivers* as well as cisterns;

we take a *watering*-pot and save a few plants from perishing. A few good men and women of the land go forth to teach the heathen; God, when the time came to deliver the Irish people from their oppressors, sent them forth to the plentiful land reserved for them here, where they till and *are tilled*. Their children will melt into our population, in which there must be an amalgamation of various elements, the calculating, cold, intellectual Saxon, the metaphysical, patient German, the vivacious, imaginative, indefinite, changeful, uncertain Celt, the superstitious Northman, the fervent children of the South. A strange compound must come out of this. There is support for all living nature—the "finest of the wheat" for the basis, and sour and sweet, and spice and spirit—a "De'il's bro"[10] it will be—or ambrosia for the gods, a perfecting and consummation of the species.

But I am far enough off from our family history, or rather my own story, which I began with; but fearing, dear Alice, that you would never know how I came here, that is to say anything farther back in the ages than dear "Father Charles," I have, and shall transmit to you all that I know of my progenitors. My father, Theodore Sedgwick, was educated at Yale College, New Haven. He was supported there by the generous efforts and sacrifices of his elder brother John. The family fortunes seem to have run out pretty much after the death of the commissioner or governor sent by Cromwell to the island of Jamaica, and after being fixed at West Hartford, [Connecticut] for two generations, my grandfather, one, I believe, of a large family, removed to Cornwall, and purchased a large farm on its bleak hills. He opened a "store" there, and, just arrived in *mezzo camino* [in the middle of the journey of life] he died of apoplexy and left three sons and three daughters. Uncle John was head of the house, and at once resolving, with my grandmother's earnest and ready coöperation, to maintain my father at college, he opened a tavern to obtain money which could not be worked out of the stony land of Cornwall. My father pursued his

---

[10] Devil's brew.

studies to the last year, when, being a party in some boyish gayeties quite outside of the Puritan tolerance of the times, he was expelled by President Stiles, of whom I received the impression, I cannot say with what accuracy, that he was a compound of pedagogue and granny.[11] My father, sobered by this cloud, took to divinity, and went to Dr. Bellamy's to study theology.[12] The doctor, I rather think, from the current anecdotes of the time, had considerable sympathy with the secular side of my father's character. At any rate, with [Doctor Bellamy's] entire sympathy and approbation, my father turned from divinity to law, and began and finished his legal studies with Mark Hopkins, of Great Barrington [Massachusetts], a distinguished lawyer of his time, and grandfather of the present President of Williams College.[13]

My father used to tell with much gusto of Dr. Bellamy that one of his parishioners, who was a notorious scamp, came to him, saying, in the parlance of the divinity that pervaded this part of New England at that period, "I feel that I have obtained a hope!" The doctor looked surprised. "I realize that I am the chief of sinners," continued the hypocritical canter. "Your neighbors have long been of that opinion," rejoined the doctor. The man went on to say out the lesson—"I feel willing to be damned for the glory of God." "Well, my friend, I don't know any one who has the slightest objection!"

I heard yesterday, while on a visit to my dear friend, Dr. [Orville]

[11]Sedgwick entered Yale College with the class of 1765. Before graduation, he was expelled by Thomas Clap, not by Ezra Stiles, who did not assume office until 1778. Sedgwick finally received his degree in 1772.

[12]Immediately after his graduation from Yale College in 1735, Joseph Bellamy (1719–1790) spent two years studying theology with Jonathan Edwards, the 18th century's most prominent theologian. Edwards's Calvinistic imprint lasted throughout Bellamy's long ministry in Bethlehem, Connecticut. Publications such as *True Religion Delineated* brought him prominence and a steady stream of students who undertook preparation for the ministry with him. Nearly all of them stayed longer than Theodore Sedgwick.

[13]Mark Hopkins (1739–1776) was Great Barrington's leading lawyer in the decade before the Revolution. Deeply involved in the protests that culminated in the separation from England, he served as a brigade major and died during the war. His grandson, also named Mark Hopkins, served as president of Williams College from 1836 to 1872.

Dewey, at Sheffield, another equally characteristic story of this old friend of my father.[14] One of his Church was up before that solemn tribunal for some profane words spoken in wrath. He was a man liable to be provoked to a sudden gust of passion by a scamp, but tender and cherishing as a June dew to the widow and fatherless. After hearing the evidence of his accusers, Dr. Bellamy said, "The poor man is a grievous sinner on one side, but my friends, I think he has more of the milk of human kindness in his heart than all the rest of my Church together!"

My father appreciated highly Mr. [Mark] Hopkins's talents and virtues, and always spoke of him as a man "comme il y a un peu" [a rare sort of man]. Like other patriotic civilians, Mr. Hopkins took up arms during the Revolutionary War. An old man, a soldier of that time—a pensioner of ours—told me the following anecdote. Mr. Hopkins had a command at White Plains, or in that vicinity, when the British were in great force near them. News came that he was ill (I believe of the disease of which he afterward prematurely died). My father went to him at great personal risk, for the British were advancing, and our people retreating. He procured a litter and soldiers—my informant was one of them—and Mr. Hopkins was placed on the litter and hastily carried off. They heard firing; Mr. Hopkins, weakened by illness, was terrified, sure he should be taken prisoner, or they should all be shot. He implored my father with tears to leave him to his fate and save himself. My father of course resisted, cheered and sustained him, and conveyed him to a place of safety. My father afterward married the young half-sister of Mark Hopkins's wife, Pamela Dwight, my beloved and tenderly remembered mother.

[14]Fourth president of the American Unitarian Association, Orville Dewey (1794–1882) served as minister for New York City's Second Unitarian Church from 1835 to 1848. During the winters that she spent in New York City, Sedgwick attended his services. Dewey also maintained a residence in Sheffield, Massachusetts, a town only a short distance from Stockbridge. Dewey's daughter, Mary E. Dewey, published *The Life and Letters of Catharine M. Sedgwick*, a selection from Sedgwick's autobiography, letters, and journals in 1872.

My father first opened an office in Barrington (Bryant,[15] the poet, occupied it afterward), and I have heard him say that for six weeks he sat looking up and down the street, like poor Dennis Bludgruddery, for a client, but no client came, and he took down his sign and moved off to Sheffield, where he began his honorable legal career. He married, before he was twenty-one, Eliza Mason, a relative of the late celebrated Jeremiah Mason.[16] She died within the year of their marriage, of smallpox, which she caught from my father. It was the practice of those times in our rural districts to shut patients ill with this hideous disease in a hospital (some little shanty set apart, out of the village, and called the pock-house) till they were pronounced beyond the possibility of communicating it. My father, thus certified, went home to his young wife. She was in a condition that made it imprudent to take inoculation. It was believed that she caught [the disease] from combing my father's hair, which he [wore] long and tied in a cue, according to the fashion of the times.[17]

My father, through life, cherished the most tender recollections of this poor lady. Not long after her death, he was lying upon the bed he had shared with her (a "field bedstead," with a bar across the two foot-posts), and unable to sleep; he said to himself, "If I could but see her as she was, in her everyday dress—see her once more, I should be comforted." (Oh, how many of us, Alice, would give the world for that one sight more, one look, one word!) Well, he pondered on this thought till suddenly the room filled with a

[15]William Cullen Bryant (1794–1878) and Catharine Maria Sedgwick became friends shortly after he published *Thanatopsis* in 1817. The support and encouragement she and her brother Harry offered were important in the early stages of Bryant's career as a poet and editor.

[16]Lawyer and politician Jeremiah Mason (1768–1848) had a highly visible legal practice in New Hampshire and Massachusets. He was equally successful in politics, serving as representative in New Hampshire's legislature and as one of the state's U.S. senators from 1813 to 1817. Eliza Mason Sedgwick was his aunt. Ironically, both Jeremiah and Eliza were the descendants of John Mason, one of the leaders in Massachusetts Bay's military expedition against the Pequods during the 1630s. Sedgwick's third novel, *Hope Leslie*, was a revisionist indictment of the Puritans' efforts to destroy this Indian tribe.

[17]It was Eliza Mason Sedgwick's pregnancy that made inoculation dangerous. Eight months pregnant when she contracted smallpox, Eliza died before giving birth.

light—not like the light of lamp, not like a thousand, the brightest—not like the light of the sun, but a heavenly radiance, and his wife—his young wife, her face lit with love and happiness, stood leaning over the bar at the foot of his bed, looking on him. He raised himself on his elbow; he wondering, surveyed her from head to foot, and fantastically, and as we sometimes do in our strongest emotions [observe trifles], he [re]marked the buckles in her shoes—he sprang forward to embrace her—she was gone—the light was gone—it was a dream. "If I had one particle of superstition," he would say, "I should believe that my wife had appeared to me!" And yet I think my dear father had that particle of superstition, for through his whole life he had once a year a dream that was like a visitation of this girl-wife. She always came to restore to him those days of young romantic love—the passages of after life vanished. I can well remember the sweet, tender expression of my father's face when he used to say, "I have had my dream!"

I do not know precisely the period that elapsed between my father's first marriage and his second one to my mother. It was not long—not much more, I think, than the canonized "year and a day."[18] In that time marriage was essential to a man's life. There were no arrangements independent of it, no substitutions for it, and, besides, my father was domestic in his disposition, out-and-out social; he could not endure solitude unless he were intensely absorbed in business, and he married. My mother was the only daughter of Brigadier Colonel Dwight and my grandmother, who had been the widow of the excellent missionary Sergeant. My mother's family (of this I have rather an indefinite impression than any knowledge) objected to my father on the score of family, they priding themselves on their gentle blood; but as he afterward rose far beyond their highest watermark, the objection was cast into oblivion by those who made it.

Their union was a very perfect one: reverence, devotion, with

---

[18]Theodore Sedgwick actually married Pamela Dwight in 1774, three years after Eliza's death. He had deferred his second marriage two years more than the customary year after the death of a spouse.

infinite tenderness on her side; respect, confidence, and unswerving love on his. Their eldest child was called, at my mother's request, Eliza Mason, after the first wife—a proof how generous and unjealous she was.

I have just (October 6, 1853) come into possession of some old letters which have carried me back deep into the interests of my parents' lives, and to give you, my dear child, some notion of my mother's character, her wisdom, her conjugal devotion, and self-negation, I copy a letter she wrote to my father at a time when he was to decide whether to continue in public life or retire from it.[19] His continuance involved his absence from her during the winter, when, with very delicate health and a nervous temperament, she must be left for many months in this cold northern country, with young children, a large household, and complicated concerns, and the necessity of economy. A distance of two hundred eighty miles— hence to Philadelphia—was a very different affair from what it would be now. The winter journey, if most prosperous, would occupy five or six days, and might twice or thrice that time, so that it was nearly as grave a question as it would be now whether a husband were to pass his winters in London. N.B. There is in the style a deference not common in these days, and you will observe, too, an old-fashioned form of expression.

> Pardon me, my dearest Mr. Sedgwick, if I beg you once more to think over the matter before you embark for life in public business. I grant that the 'call of our country,' 'the voice of Fame,' and 'the Honorable,' 'Right Honorable' are high-sounding words. 'They play around the head, but come not near the heart.' A wish to serve the true interests of our country is certainly a laudable ambition, but the intention brings many cares with it. You best know what they are, as you had had a large share of them already.
>
> The new government is yet untried. If I mistake not, the success of it depends more on the virtue and economy of the people than on the wisdom of those who govern, or the uncommon excellency that is supposed to attend the form.

[19]The letters of Pamela Dwight Sedgwick and other members of the family are deposited at the Massachusetts Historical Society.

Should the people find they are not happy under it, the fault will all be in their rulers. They will be subjected to the envy of some, the reproach of others, and the remarks of all. The interest of your family deserves some attention. Men in public life are generally dependent in more senses than one. Should you find your circumstances straitened at a future day, I know, from the tender affection you have for your children, it would give you great pain. A return to Congress would then be painful, and would be thought degrading. On my own account I will say nothing [but] that I have not a distant wish you should sacrifice your happiness to mine, or your inclination to my opinion. If, on the whole, you think a public line of life will be most conducive to your interest and happiness, I will pray that He alone who is the author of all good will strew peace in all your paths. Submission is my duty, and, however hard, I will try to practice what reason teaches me I am under obligation to do. Pamela Sedgwick.[20]

My father decided for public life, and I believe my mother never again expressed one word of remonstrance or dissatisfaction. She, no doubt, was gratified with his honorable public career, inasmuch as it proved his worth, but I think she had no sympathy with what is called honor and distinction; she was essentially modest and humble, and she *looked beyond.*

She was oppressed with cares and responsibilities; her health failed; she made no claims; she uttered no complaints; she knew she was most tenderly beloved, and held in the very highest respect by my father. But her physical strength was not equal to the demands on her, and her reason gave way. She had two or three turns of insanity, which lasted each, I believe, some months; I know not how long, for I was too young to remember anything but being told that my "mamma was sick, and sent away to a good doctor." This physician, I have since learned, was a Dr. Waldo, of Richmond, [Massachusetts] who took my mother to his house, and was supposed to treat her judiciously and most kindly. But oh! I cannot bear to think—it has been one of the saddest sorrows of my life to

---

[20]At the top of the last page of Pamela's letter, Catharine Sedgwick wrote: "A beautiful and characteristic letter from my beloved mother, wise and tender." See Pamela Dwight Sedgwick to Theodore Sedgwick, Sedgwick IV, 18 Nov. [179?].

think how much aggravated misery my dear, gentle, patient mother must have suffered from the ignorance of the right mode of treating mental diseases which then existed.

My mother may have had a constitutional tendency to insanity, but I believe the delicate construction of a sensitive and reserved temperament, a constitution originally delicate, and roughly handled by the medical treatment of the times, and the terrible weight of domestic cares, will sufficiently account for her mental illness without supposing a cerebral tendency which her descendants may have inherited. But this fear may be wholesome to them, if it lead them to a careful physical training, to guarding against nervous susceptibilities and weakness, and to avoiding the stimulants and excitements so unfavorable to nervous constitutions. I firmly believe that people may be educated out of a hereditary tendency to insanity more surely than one can eradicate a liability to consumption, or any other scrofulous poison.

I am sure my father felt throughout his public career an harassing sense of the suffering it occasioned my mother. In a letter to my sisters, then young girls, dated 1791, three years after the letter I have quoted from, he says,

> You can imagine how much the conflict between a sense of public duty and private inclination affected my spirits and temper while I was at home. I most sincerely endeavored to weigh all circumstances, and to discover what I ought to do. This I believed I did, but the struggle was severe and painful. The description you give of her patience and resignation is precisely such as I should have expected. You know not, my dear children, the blessing of having such a parent. While she possesses all the softness and tenderness which renders woman so amiable, she has a greatness and nobleness of mind which I have hardly known equaled by her sex. How dignified, how exemplary in all her sufferings!

In the same letter he says,

> This life is a checkered scene. I myself have been what is called a prosperous man.[21] I have reason to bless God I have been less unfor-

[21]In the margin Catharine added: "Then forty-six years old."

tunate, even in my own opinion, than many others. To the view of the world, I have been, I doubt not, an object of envy. Connected with one of the best of women, blessed with *many* children, all hopeful, and those who have become more advanced of good characters and deserving them, in easy circumstances, respectable in my profession, honored in my own country, and known and respected in others, yet I feel that this life is far from affording felicity. How important is it, then, that our hopes should not rest in these things! May, my dear children, that gracious Being, whose goodness has done better for me than I deserved, be the kind protector and guardian of my beloved offspring, most fervently prays your ever affectionate papa, Theodore Sedgwick.

I had in my hand yesterday too another of my father's letters, which may entertain you at the distance of time you live from the dynasty of Washington, for it is "sixty years since."

Philadelphia 1794—I dined yesterday at the President's, where I was treated with a distinguished partiality very grateful to my feelings. The President, you know, never sits at the head of his table. That place he particularly requested me to take; Mr. Dandridge, as usual, sat at the other end. When Mrs. Washington retired, she stopped and desired me not to go away until I had been entertained by *Nelly's* playing. Accordingly, I went up stairs, and the good lady requested me to take a seat on the sofa by her. She then asked if I had any particular tune which was a favorite with me, and added, "*For Nelly can play any thing.*"[22] Submitting myself to her taste, to prevent discovering that I had none,[23] Nelly played several grave and solemn tunes, and accompanied them inimitably with her voice. Mrs. Washington, perceiving me unusually solemn, turned to Miss Custis and said, with her usual amiable simplicity, "Nelly, play for Mr. Sedgwick 'Chase away dull care' don't you see he wants to be enlivened?" After spending with the good family an hour, I accompanied them to a concert for the benefit of a French family.

These were victims of the Revolution, and he goes on to detail particulars of several of them in Philadelphia, among others the

[22]Eleanor Custis (Nelly) was the daughter of Martha Custis Washington and her first husband, Daniel Parke Custis.
[23]In the margin Catharine added: "like father like children."

Duke de Liancourt and the Bishop of Autun.[24] But we, in our day, are more familiar with the reception of exiles than my father was, and you and your contemporaries, dear Alice, are like[ly] to have the opportunity of a like hospitality.

I copy for you a little letter written by my father to his eldest child [Eliza] when she was a little girl of ten years. It is a fair sample of the fond, tender letters he was in the habit of writing periodically and punctually to his children while he was immersed in the most important national affairs.

> Accept my thanks, my kind and good child, for your kind and pretty letter by Mr. E. Believe me, my sweet prattler, that you can not, more than I do, regret our separation. Should it so happen that my duty will permit, I will fly on the wings of Love to see and embrace my lovely, sweet children. If you knew how happy I was made by the information that you are a good child, you would not fail to continue to be so. I do not believe you will. I should be miserable if I did. Remember, my love, that our happiness or our misery depends chiefly on our good conduct, and you will not fail to endeavor to be good. Be kind to your mamma. She is good. She deserves all your attention. Remember that you are the eldest child, and that you can reward your parents' care by a good example. Farewell. I heartily pray God to make you virtuous and happy.

In all his letters he expresses the most thoughtful love for my mother, the highest appreciation of her character. When fearing a recurrence of her mental malady, he says, "Read to her, or persuade her to read diverting books. Every other object must submit to an attention to her. Is company diverting, she must be indulged with it. Does it increase her gloom, it must be kept from her. She is the

---

[24]Deeply loyal to Louis XVI, the Duc de Liancourt (1747–1827) kept his titles but little else during the French Revolution. He fled to England after the collapse of the monarchy early in the 1790s and spent the rest of the decade there and in the United States before he returned to France. The Bishop of Autun from 1789 to 1791, Charles Talleyrand (1754–1838) was more fortunate. Remembered for the central role he played in France's politics from the French Revolution until his death 40 years later, the briefly exiled Talleyrand spent the years from 1793 to 1795 in the United States before returning to France and becoming the country's foreign minister.

best of human beings, and every circumstance of business or of pleasure must be made to submit to her restoration."

I have been reading a mass of my father's letters from 1784 to 1789, addressed to my sister Eliza and to my mother. My sister Eliza resembled my mother much more than Frances or myself. She had her modesty, her self-diffidence, her humility. This was a constitutional quality, but so authorized and enforced by their religion that to them both it took the potent form of a duty. I rather think that my mother was intellectually superior to my sister; if not originally, by the long partnership with a superior mind occupied in great affairs. Her long separations from my father seem to have been almost cruel to her. He continually laments over them, and, but that his compunction is tempered by the conviction of an overruling duty to his country, he would have been miserable. Her sufferings are past, and, I doubt not, prepared her to enjoy more keenly the rest and felicities of heaven. The good done by my father in contributing to establish the government, and to swell the amount of that political virtue which makes the history of the Federal party the record of the purest patriotism the world has known—*that remains.*

You do not seem now, my dear little Alice, like one who will ever be curious to inquire into the shades of political virtue; but who knows but you may some bright day to come have a son who will be prying into his ancestral history, and whose pulses will beat quicker for the testimony I give to my father's earnest devotion to his country.

I was a child at the period of the great ferment occasioned by the decline of the Federal party and the growth of the Democratic party. My father had the habit of having his children always about him, and we had so strong a sympathy with him that there was no part of his life which we did not partake. I remember well looking upon a Democrat as an enemy to his country, and at the party as sure, if it prevailed, to work its destruction. I heard my father's conversation with his political friends, and in the spontaneous expressions of domestic privacy, and I received the impression then (and, looking back with a riper judgement, I feel assured of its correctness) that the Federal party loved their country, and were devoted to it, as virtuous parents are to their children. It was to my father what selfish men's private affairs are to them, of deep and ever-present interest. It was not the success of men, or the acquisition of office, but the maintenance of principles on which, as it appeared to them, the sound health and true life of their country depended. They dreaded French influence—they believed Jefferson to be false, the type[25] of all evil—they were a good deal influenced by old prestiges—they retained their predilections for Great Britain. They hoped a republic might exist and prosper, and be the happiest government in the world, but not without a strong aristocratic element; and that the constitutional monarchy of Britain was the safest and happiest government on earth, I am sure they believed. But while they admired the monarchical government of Great Britain they were firm to the experiment of the Republic and had no treasonable thoughts of introducing a monarchy here.

Their misfortune, and perhaps the inevitable consequence of having been educated loyal subjects of a monarchical government, was a thorough distrust of "the people." I remember my father, one of the kindest-hearted of men, and most observant of the rights of all beneath him, habitually spoke politically of the people as "Jacobins," "sans-culottes," and "miscreants." He—and in this I speak of him as the type of the Federal party—dreaded every upward step they made, regarding elevation as a depression, in proportion to their ascension of the intelligence and virtue of the country. The upward tendencies from education, and improvements in the arts of life, were unknown to them. They judged of the "people" as they had been, as [they] were the "greasy, unwashed multitude" of Rome and of Shakespeare's time—as they are now for the most part in Europe, utterly inexperienced in government, incapable of attaining to its abstractions, or feeling its moralities.

My father felt it to be his duty to remain in public life at every

[25]Epitome.

64

private sacrifice—at the expense of his domestic happiness, his home-love, which was his ruling passion. I know he must have felt the craving that all men conscious of power feel for enlarging the bounds of their horizon. The Miltons are not content to be "inglorious," nor the Hampdens to be "mere villagers."[26] Still I feel sure that nothing short of a self-devotion to his country's good would have induced him to leave my mother, winter after winter, tottering under her burden of care, and so far separate himself from his little children, whose lisping voices seemed to follow him, and whose loved images were ever about him. Nothing can exceed the unintermitting tenderness of his letters to my mother. He never failed, in any pressure of business, to write to her and to his children. How well do I remember the arrival of those packets! The mail came but once a week, and then we all gathered about our mother, each expecting, and very often each receiving, a letter "from papa!" I can see them now—the form of the letters—the directions, as they looked then. I *do* see them now, time-worn and discolored, but still imbued with the essence of my father's soul. No man was in his affections a truer image of Him "who is love."

My mother, after years of decline from a life of ill health, died in 1807, at the age of fifty-four. The portrait I have of her was as faithful a likeness as so wretched a painting could be. Bad as it is, it will give you an impression of her personal dignity, and of the sweetness and sensibility of her character, and of her temperament, which, if not originally a sad one, became melancholy from her tragic personal trials.

I will copy here a character of her, written, I think, by my brother Harry. It has a little of the stiffness of an unaccustomed pen, and the formality of an obituary, but it was true to the letter, which few obituaries are.

---

[26]The poet and pamphleteer John Milton (1608–1674) and the Parliamentary leader John Hampden (1594–1643) were prominent supporters of the Puritans during the English Civil Wars. Milton also became a civil servant during Oliver Cromwell's Commonwealth.

Mrs. Pamela Sedgwick: In attempting to offer a tribute to her memory, the author feels the most trembling solicitude. That eulogium, which ought to have been kept sacred to eminent merit, has been so prostituted to vulgar use and on unworthy occasions, that there remain no terms by which to distinguish such virtue as was that of this most excellent woman.

Through a whole lifetime she never once expressed a feeling of impatience. Such was the strength of her submissive piety; but, from the sensibility of her temper, she was often afflicted with the severest anguish, from an apprehension that her life was useless.

She seemed sweetly to repose on the pillow of Faith, and, when tortured by pain and debilitated by disease, she not only sustained herself, but was the comfort, support, and delight of her family.

Her sufferings, in degree and duration, have been perhaps without a parallel, but they reached not the measure of her faith and her patience. Had she endured less, she would never have exhibited, and her friends could never have estimated, the invincible meekness and the gentleness of her heavenly temper. It may not be profane or irreverent to suppose that, with some distant resemblance to our Redeemer, she did not suffer solely for herself—that her trials and her piety were in some measure designed for the instruction of others; and we may be permitted to hope that her example and her memory, by their influence on the heart and the conduct, will contribute to the eternal welfare of those she most loved. Many whom she has instructed in the spirit and practice of the holy religion she professed, and many whose wants and pains have been relieved by her bounty and soothed by her attention, will gratefully acknowledge that this is but a faint delineation of her virtue, and their tears will confess that, though the sketch is imperfect, it is not false.

What her friends, and, above all, what her husband and children have suffered, must be left to the conception of the reader—it *cannot be told*. But it is hoped that they will try to dismiss all selfish regards, and to rejoice that she is now where the righteous have their reward, and the weary are at rest. Stockbridge, September 1807.

Beloved mother! Even at this distance of time, the thought of what I suffered when you died thrills my soul!

My father felt the solitariness of his home. He was the sort of man to whom the companionship of a woman is a necessity. He married again, a little more than a year after my mother's death,

Penelope Russell, a Boston woman, of a highly respectable family, an agreeable exterior, and an attractive vivacity. My father was flattered into this marriage by some good-natured friends who believed he would be the happier for it, and knew she would. Like most second marriages where there are children, it was disastrous. The poor lady was put into a life for which she was totally unfitted. She knew nothing of the business of country domestic life, and her ambition to shine in it was simply ludicrous to us—onerous to her. She fluttered gracefully enough through the inanities of town drawingrooms, but the reality and simplicity of our country life was insupportable to her. We were all matured; I was eighteen, Charles sixteen, the rest all married or away from home. But I forget, dear Alice, that I began with telling you the story of my own life, and that I shall come, in due time, to this chapter of its experience.

I was born, then, in 1789, December 28, in a bitter cold night, as I have heard my Aunt Dwight say, who was present on the occasion. It was in the southwest room of the dear old house, that which your Aunt Susan [Ridley Sedgwick] now occupies as her parlor. Your "father Charles" was born two years after, in December 1791. I came into the world two months before I was due. It was owing to this, probably, that I had the delicacy of complexion which made my good uncle, Dr. Sergeant, and *Mumbet* remember me as "fair and handsome as a London doll." I know nothing memorable of my infancy except that my sister Eliza, through all that cold winter, slept in the room with my mother, and got up in the cold watches of the night to feed me, my mother being unable to nurse me. What such a love-service was those only can estimate who remember our houses before the winter atmosphere was tempered by stoves.

How faint and few are the recollections of a childhood that flowed smoothly on the current of love! I remember my first attempting to say "Theodore" and "Philadelphia," and I remember a trick I had of biting the glass from which I was drinking, and, from a comparison of dates, this was within the first two years of my life. Now, my darling, don't think I am superannuated because I think it worth while to record this. It is associated with my first impression of my father. I remember that there was company at table—Miss Susan Morton, from New York, the grandmother of Mary Quincy whom you know. I remember where she sat, where my father sat, and where I sat. I recall *perfectly* the feeling with which I turned my eye to him, expecting to see that brow (which all his life long marked to me the state of his feelings as distinctly as the degrees on a thermometer do the state of the weather) cloud with displeasure, but it was smooth as love could make it. That consciousness, that glance, that assurance remained stamped indelibly—and I think I have never known a greater fear than to see a cloud on that brow.

How trivial, too, are the recollections of childhood! The next notch on my memory is of being sent over to Mrs. Caroline Dwight (the predecessor of your grandmother *Wight*) to borrow a boy's dress of Frank Dwight's, which was to be the model of your "father Charles's" first male attire. Then come thronging recollections of my childhood, its joys and sorrows— "Papa's going away," and "Papa's coming home;" the dreadful clouds that came over our sunny home when mamma was sick; my love of Mumbet, that noble woman, the main pillar of our household; distinctly the faces of the favorite servants, *Grippy*, Sampson Derby, Sampson the cook, a runaway slave, "Lady Prime," and various others who, to my mind's eye, are still young, vigorous, and alert! Not Agrippa, for him I saw through the various stages of manhood to decrepit old age. Grippy is one of the few who will be immortal in our village annals. He enlisted in the army of the Revolution, and, being a very well-trained and adroit servant, he was taken into the personal service of the noble Pole, Kosciuszko.[27] Unlike most heroes, he always re-

---

[27]Intrigued by the prospect of a colonial revolt against England, Tadeusz Andrzej Bonawentura Kosciuszko (1746–1817) arrived in America one month after independence had been declared. He immediately volunteered and served in the Continental Army until the end of the conflict. Kosciuszko was also involved in the Polish uprisings against Russia. He later returned to the United States and in 1797 was paid the $15,000 due him and granted 500 acres of land in Ohio. Given his demeaning treatment of Agrippa, it is ironic that the profits from the land sold after his death were used to establish the Colored School in Newark, New Jersey, one of the earliest educational institutions for African Americans.

mained a hero to his valet Grippy, who many a time has charmed our childhood with stories of his soldier-master.

One I remember, of which the catastrophe moved my childish indignation. Kosciuszko was absent from camp, and Agrippa, to amuse his fellow-servants, dressed in his master's most showy uniform, and blacked with shining black-ball his legs and feet to resemble boots. Just as he was in full exhibition, his master returned, and, resolved to have his own fun out of the joke, he bade "Grip" follow him, and took him to the tents of several officers, introducing him as an African prince. Poor Grippy, who had as mortal an aversion practically as our preachers of temperance have theoretically to every species of spirituous liquor, was received at each new introduction by a soldier's hospitality, and compelled, by a nod from his master, to taste each abhorrent cup, brandy, or wine, or "Hollands,"[28] or whatever (to Grippy poisonous) potion it might chance to be, till, when his master was sated with the joke, he gave him a kick, and sent him staggering away.

I think Grippy was fully compensated by the joke for the ignominy of its termination. He had a fund of humor and mother-wit, and was a sort of Sancho Panza in the village, always trimming other men's follies with a keen perception, and the biting wit of wisdom.[29] Grippy was a capital subaltern, but a very poor officer. As a servant he was faultless, but in his own domain at home a tyrant. Mumbet (Mah Bet), on the contrary, though absolutely perfect in service, was never servile. Her judgment and will were never subordinated by mere authority; but when she went to her own little home, like old Eli,[30] she was the victim of her affections, and was weakly indulgent to her riotous and ruinous descendants. I be-

[28]"Hollands," a Dutch gin distilled from rye and barley and flavored with juniper, was a popular drink in Revolutionary America.

[29]The companion of the titular hero in Miguel de Cervantes *Don Quixote*, Sancho Panza embodied the common sense, shrewdness, and wit that Sedgwick ascribed to Agrippa. Panza's characteristics served as a foil for Quixote's idealism.

[30]The Biblical priest and judge Eli provided a telling example of a parent whose devotion to children clashed with public obligations. Despite the greed and immorality displayed by Haphni and Phinehas, Eli only chided his sons. Eli's failure to punish them led to his downfall and their deaths.

lieve, my dear Alice, that the people who surround us in our child-hood, whose atmosphere infolds us, as it were, have more to do with the formation of our characters than all our didactic and pre-ceptive education. Mumbet had a clear and nice perception of jus-tice, and a stern love of it, an uncompromising honesty in word and deed, and conduct of high intelligence, that made her the un-conscious moral teacher of the children she tenderly nursed. She was a remarkable exception to the general character of her race. Injustice and oppression have confounded their moral sense, cheated as they have been of their liberty, defrauded at wholesale of time and strength, what wonder that they allow themselves petty reprisals—a sort of predatory warfare in the households of their masters or employers—for, though they now among us be free, they retain the vices of a degraded and subjected people.

I do not believe that any amount of temptation could have in-duced Mumbet to swerve from truth. She knew nothing of the com-promises of timidity, or the overwrought conscientiousness of big-otry. Truth was her nature—the offspring of courage—truth and loyalty. In my childhood I clung to her with instinctive love and faith, and the more I know and observe of human nature, the higher does she rise above others, whatever may have been their instruc-tion or accomplishment. In her the image of her Maker was cast in material so hard and pure that circumstances could not alter its outline or cloud its lustre. This may seem rhodomontade[31] to you, my child. "Why," you may exclaim, "my aunt could say nothing more of Washington, and this woman was once a slave, born a slave, and always a servant!" Yes, so she was, and yet I well remember that during her last sickness, when I daily visited her in her little hut—her then independent home—I said then, and my sober after judg-ment ratified it, that I felt awed as if I had entered the presence of Washington. Even protracted suffering and mortal sickness, with

[31]Boastful.

70

old age, could not break down her spirit. When Dr. F.[32] said to her, with the proud assurance of his spiritual office, "Are you not afraid to meet your God?" "No, sir," she replied, "I am not afeard. I have tried to do my duty, and I am *not* afeard!" This was truth, and she spoke it with calm dignity. Creeds crumble before such a Faith. Speaking to me of the mortal nature of her disease, she said, "It is the last stroke, and it is the best stroke."

Her expressions of feeling were simple and comprehensive. When she suddenly lost a beloved grandchild, ("Lydia Maria") the only descendant of whom she had much hope—she was a young mother, and died without an instant's warning—I remember Mumbet walking up and down the room with her hands knit together and great tears rolling down her cheeks, repeating, as if to send back into her soul its swelling sorrow, "Don't say a word; it's God's will!" And when I was sobbing over my dead mother, she said, "We must be quiet. Don't you think I am grieved? Our hair has grown white together." Even at this distance of time I remember the effect on me of her still, solemn sadness. Elsewhere, my dear, you will see notices of the memorable things in her life, and I need not here repeat them. Her virtues are recorded, with a truth that few epitaphs can boast, on the stone we placed over her grave. Your "father Charles" wrote the inscription.[33]

Among my earliest recollections is that of my particular and par-

---

[32]David Dudley Field (1781–1867) served as the minister for Stockbridge's Congregationalists from 1819 to 1837. Field also compiled a *History of the County of Berkshire, Massachusetts* (1829).

[33]Although she cites Charles as the author, evidence in the family's papers suggests that Sedgwick herself wrote the inscription. In a letter written five days after Elizabeth Freeman's death on 28 Dec. 1829, Charles informed his sister that their beloved Mumbet had died, adding "I wish you would send me the epitaph as soon as you conveniently can." The inscription deposited in the papers is also in Sedgwick's hand. It is as follows: "ELIZABETH FREEMAN. Known by the name of Mumbet. Died December 28, 1829. Her supposed age was eighty-five years. She could neither read nor write, yet in her own sphere, she had no superior or equal. She neither wasted time nor property. She never violated a trust, nor failed to perform a duty. In every situation of domestic trial she was the most efficient helper and the tenderest friend. Good mother, farewell." See Sedgwick IV, Massachusetts Historical Society.

amount love for your Uncle Robert. Once, when ransacking the barn with my brothers for eggs, a new and half finished barn, I somehow slipped under a mass of hay, and was so oppressed by it, and so scared, that I could scarcely make a sound. Robert heard my faint cries, but could not find me, and he ran to call my father, who, with some friends who happened to be with him, soon extricated me. From their caresses and conversation I inferred that my danger of suffocation had been imminent, and I looked henceforward upon my favorite brother as my preserver. He was more than any other my protector and companion. Charles was as near my own age, but he was younger, and a feeling of dependence—of most loving dependence—on Robert began then, which lasted through his life. I remember once when I was ill, and not more than five years old, his refusing to go out and play with "the boys," and lying down by me to soothe and amuse me. How early we are impressed by love and disinterestedness!

My dear Alice, I wish I could give you a true picture, and a vivid one, of my *fragmentary* childhood—how different from the thoughtful, careful (whether judicious or injudicious) education of the present day.

"Education" in the common sense I had next to none, but there was much chance seed dropped in the fresh furrow, and some of it was good seed, and some of it, I may say, fell on good ground. My father was absorbed in political life, but his affections were at home. My mother's life was eaten up with calamitous sicknesses. My sisters were just at that period when girls' eyes are dazzled with their own glowing future. I had constantly before me examples of goodness, and from all sides admonitions to virtue, but no regular instruction. I went to the district schools, or, if any other school a little more select or better chanced, I went to that. But no one dictated my studies or overlooked my progress. I remember feeling an intense ambition to be at the head of my class, and generally being there. Our minds were not weakened by too much study—reading, spelling, and Dwight's Geography were the only paths of knowledge into which we were led. Yes, I did go in a slovenly way through the four first rules of arithmetic, and learned the names of the several parts of speech, and could parse glibly.

At eleven I went to New York and had the very best teaching of an eminent Professor of Dancing!—Monsieur Lalliet. When I think that then there was but one accepted French dancing master in New York where now there are nearly a million inhabitants, I feel as if I had been on the earth as long as the Wandering Jew! [And I] had a French master who came three times a week, and who to my brother Robert's infinite amusement, complimented my "grande apprehension," but who, as far as I can recollect, taught me nothing, because, as I imagine, I preferred reading pleasant books, and being petted by pleasant people, to the task of getting lessons. My sister was confined that winter with her first child, and I had no one to control me, or see after me.

But my childhood here in Stockbridge was a most happy one. I enjoyed unrestrained the pleasures of a rural childhood; I went with herds of school-girls nutting, and berrying, and bathing by moonlight, and wading by daylight in the lovely Housatonic that flows through my father's meadows. I saw its beauty then; I loved it as a playfellow; I loved the hills and mountains that I roved over. My father was an observer and lover of nature, my sister Frances a romantic, passionate devotee to it, and if I had no natural perception or relish of its loveliness, I caught it from them, so that my heart was early knit to it, and I at least early studied and early learned this picture language, so rich and universal.

From my earliest recollection to this day of our Lord, 13th of October, 1853, nature has been an ever fresh and growing beauty and enjoyment to me; and now, when so many of my dearest friends are gone, when few even of my contemporaries are left, when new social pleasures have lost their excitement, the sun coming up over these hills and sinking behind them—the springing and the dying year—all changes and aspects of nature are more beautiful to me than ever. They have more solemnity, perhaps, but it is because they have more meaning. If they speak in a lower tone to my dimmed eye-sight, it is a gentler and tenderer one.

What would the children now, who are steeped to the lips in "olo-gies," think of a girl of eight spending a whole summer working a wretched sampler which was not even a tolerable specimen of its species. But even as early as that, my father, whenever he was at home, kept me up and at his side till nine o'clock in the evening, to listen to him while he read aloud to the family Hume, or Shake-speare, or Don Quixote, or Hudibras![34] Certainly I did not under-stand them, but some glances of celestial light reached my soul, and I caught from his magnetic sympathy some elevation of feeling, and that love of reading which has been to me "education."

I remember a remark of Gibbon's which corresponded with my own experience. He says that the love of reading with which an aunt inspired him was worth all the rest of his education, and what must that "rest" have been in the balance against the pauperism of my in-struction![35]

I was not more than twelve years old (I think but ten) when, during one winter, I read Rollin's Ancient History.[36] The walking to our school-house was often bad, and I took my lunch (how well I remember the bread and butter, and "nut-cakes," and cold sausage, and nuts, and apples, that made the miscellaneous contents of that enchanting lunch basket), and in the interim between the morning and pm school I crept under my desk (the desks were so made as to afford little close recesses under them) and read, and munched, and forgot myself in Cyrus's greatness!

It was one [of] those pleasant winters that Crocker brought, at

---

[34]The authors Theodore Sedgwick chose included the philosopher David Hume and the dramatist William Shakespeare. He also selected Miguel de Cervantes's *Don Quixote* and Samuel Butler's *Hudibras*, a satirical poem that derides English Puritans for intol-erance, prejudice, and hypocrisy. The poem's major characters are modeled upon the famed Quixote and his companion Sancho Panza.

[35]The author of *The History of the Decline and Fall of the Roman Empire* (1776–1788), Edward Gibbon (1737–1794) was widely read on both sides of the Atlantic. Catherine Porten, the aunt who inspired Gibbon's devotion to reading, introduced him to the same 18th-century translations of Homer and Virgil that Sedgwick read during her childhood.

[36] Initially issued in English in the early 18th century, Charles Rollin's multivolume *Ancient History* was published in a variety of editions. More than 20 of these widely read editions were available by the early 19th century.

the close of the afternoon school, "old Rover" to the schoolhouse door for me to ride home. The gallant, majestic old veteran was then superannuated, and treated with all the respect that waits on age. I believe this was the hardest service he rendered then, but this made his life not quite a sinecure, for it was my custom and delight to take up my favorite school friends, one after another, and ride them home, putting old Rover to his utmost speed, and I think the poor old horse caught something of our youthful spirits, for he galloped over the plain with us, distancing the boys, who were fond of running at his heels, hurrahing and throwing up their hats.

I was a favorite with my schoolmates, partly, I fear, because I had what the phrenologists term an excessive love of approbation, and partly that I had, more than the rest, the means of gratifying them. On Saturday it was usual to appoint two of the girls to sweep the schoolhouse and set it in order, and these two chose a third. I was usually distinguished by the joint vote of my compatriots, and why? I had unlimited credit at the "store," where my father kept an open account, and, while the girls swept, I provided a lunch of Malaga wine and raisins, or whatever was to be had that suited the "sweet tooth" of childhood. I well remember my father's consternation when he looked over the semiannual bill, and found it dotted with these charges, "per daughter Catharine," in country fashion. He was much more amused than displeased, but I remember he cut me off from thereafter being in that mode "glorious" by a "my dear little girl, this must not be in future." What would our Temperance zealots say to so slight a rebuke on such an occasion! But it was effectual, and left no stinging sense of wrong, which a harsher visitation of an unconscious error would have done.

Oh, how different was my miscellaneous childhood from the driving study and the elaborate accomplishments of children of my class of the present day! I have all my life felt the want of more systematic training, but there were peculiar circumstances in my condition that in some degree supplied these great deficiencies, and these were blessings ever to be remembered with gratitude. I was reared in an atmosphere of high intelligence. My father had uncommon mental vigor. So had my brothers. Their daily habits, and pursuits, and pleasures were intellectual, and I naturally imbibed from them a kindred taste. Their talk was *not* of beeves,[37] nor of making money; that now universal passion had not entered into men and possessed them as it does now, or, if it had, it was not in the sanctuary of our home—there the money-changers did not come. My father was richer than his neighbors. His income supplied abundantly the wants of a very careless family and an unmeasured hospitality, but nothing was ever given to mere style, and nothing was wasted on vices.

I know we were all impressed with a law that no prodigalities were to be permitted, and that we were all to spend conscientiously; but our consciences were not very tender, I think, and when I look back upon the freedom of our expenditures, I wonder that the whole concern was not ruined. I don't remember that I had a silk frock before I was fourteen years old. I wore stuffs in winter (such fabrics as in the present advanced condition of manufactures a factory-girl would scarcely wear; a villainous stuff I particularly recall for school wear, called "bird's-eye"), and calicoes, and muslinets, and muslins for summer; but, thus limited in quality and variety, I was allowed any number; and I remember one winter, when I was about nine or ten, being particularly unfortunate in scorching my "bird's-eye," I bought, at my own discretion, three or four new dresses in the course of the winter. And in the article of shoes, the town-bought morocco slippers were few and far between, but I was permitted to order a pair of calf-skin shoes as often as I fancied I wanted them, and our village shoemaker told me in after life that his books showed fifteen pairs made for me in one year! No disrespect either to his fabrication or his leather; the shoes were burnt, or water-soaked, or run down at the heel—sad habits occasioned by the want of female supervision. My dear mother, most neat and orderly, was often ill or absent, my sisters were married, my father took no cognizance of such matters, and I had a natural carelessness

---

[37]Plural of beef.

which a lifetime of consciousness of its inconvenience and struggle against it has not overcome. You, dear Alice, are brought up with all the advantages of order in both your parents. But, missing this, I look back with satisfaction to the perfect freedom that set no limit to expansion.

No bickering or dissension was ever permitted. Love was the habit, the life of the household rather than the law, or rather it was the law of our nature. Neither the power of despots nor the universal legislation of our republic can touch this element, for as God is love, so love is God, is life, is light. We were born with it—it was our inheritance. But the duty and the virtue of guarding all its manifestations, of never failing in its demonstrations, of guarding its interchanges and smaller duties, was most vigilant[ly] watched, most peremptorily insisted on. A querulous tone, a complaint, a slight word of dissension, was met by that awful frown of my father's. Jove's thunder was to a pagan believer but as a summer day's drifting cloud to it. It was not so dreadful because it portended punishment—it was punishment; it was a token of a suspension of the approbation and love that were our life.

Have I given you an idea of the circumstances and education that made a family of seven children—all honorable men and women— all, I think I may say without exaggeration, having noble aspirations and strong affections, with the fixed principle that these were holy, inviolable?

I have always considered country life with outlets to the great world as an essential advantage in education. Besides all the teaching and inspiration of Nature, and the development of the faculties (in our country life) from the necessity of using them for daily exigencies, one is brought into close social relations with all conditions of people. There are no barriers between you and your neighbors. There are grades and classes in our democratic community seen and acknowledged. These must be every where, as Scott[38] truly says,

[38]The novelist Sir Walter Scott (1771–1832) was immensely popular in nineteenth-century America. Sedgwick described his influence in an entry recorded in her journal shortly after his death. See entry p. 130.

"except among the Hottentots," but with us one sees one's neighbor's private life unveiled The highest and the lowest meet in their joys and sorrows, at weddings and funerals, in sicknesses and distresses of all sorts. Not merely as alms-bearers, but the richest and highest go to the poorest to "watch" with them in sickness, and perform the most menial offices for them. And though your occupations, your mode of life may be very different from the artisan's, your neighbor, you meet him on an apparent equality, and talk with him as members of one family. In my youth there was something more of the old valuation than now. My mother's family was of the old established gentry of Western Massachusetts, connected by blood and friendship with the families of the "River-gods," as the Hawleys, Worthingtons, and Dwights of Connecticut River were then designated.[39] My father had attained an elevated position in political life, and his income was ample and liberally expended. My father was born too soon to relish the freedoms of democracy, and I have seen his brow lower when a free-and-easy mechanic came to the *front* door, and upon one occasion I remember his turning off the "east steps" doorway (I am *sure* not kicking, but the demonstration was unequivocal) a grown-up lad who kept his hat on after being told to take it off. (Would the President of the United States dare do as much now!)

But, with all this tenacious adherence to the habits of the elder times, no man in life was kindlier than my father. One of my contemporaries, now a venerable missionary, told me last summer an anecdote, perhaps worth preserving, as characterizing the times and individuals. He was a gentle boy, the son of a shoemaker, and then clerk to the clerk of the court. The boy had driven his master to Lenox, and all the way this gentleman, conscious that his dignity must be preserved by vigilance, had maintained silence. When they came to their destination, he ordered the boy to take his trunk into

[39]Members of the Connecticut River Valley's elite were commonly known as the "river gods" during the 18th century. All of the families to whom Sedgwick referred had established themselves in the Valley during the 1600s and maintained their social and political dominance throughout the next century.

the house. As he set it down in the entry, my father, then judge of the Supreme Judicial Court, was coming down stairs, bringing his trunk himself. He set it down, accosted the boy most kindly, and gave him his cordial hand. The lad's feelings, chilled by his master's haughtiness, at once melted, and took an impression of my father's kindness that was never effaced.

The Bench at the time my father was placed on it was occupied by men of surly, crusty, oppressive manners. The [members of the] Bar were in a state of antagonism, and some of them had even determined to leave their profession. My father's kind, courteous, considerate manners were said by his contemporaries to have produced an entire revolution. The children of my father, from instinct, from the example of their parents, and the principles of their home, had that teaching whose value Scott so well expressed in the "Fortunes of Nigel." "For ourselves," he says (and what does he not say better than another man—not to say any other!), "we can assure the reader—and perhaps, if we have ever been able to afford him amusement, it is owing in a great degree to this cause—that we never found ourselves in company with the stupidest of all possible companions in a post-chaise, or with the most arrant cumber-corner that ever occupied a place in a mail-coach, without finding that, in the course of our conversation with him, we had some ideas suggested to us, either grave or gay, or some information communicated in the course of our journey which we should have regretted not to have learned, and which we should have been sorry to have immediately forgotten."[40] It was the same principle by which Napoleon made himself the focus of every man's light. And in our humble, obscure village life, we profited by this "free-trade" school of ideas. There were no sacrifices made of personal dignity or purity; nor, if there was in condition or character a little elevation above the community we lived in, was it preserved by arrogant vigilance or jealous proscription.

One of the periods most marked in my childhood, and best re-

[40]Sir Walter Scott's *The Fortunes of Nigel* (1822), Ch. XXVII.

membered, because it was out of the general current of my life, was a summer when I was seven or eight years old, passed under the care of my cousin Sabrina Parsons, in Bennington, Vermont, at the house of the Rev. Mr. Swift, the husband of my father's eldest sister. There were a dozen children, more or less, some grown, some still young—the kindest and cheerfulest people in the world. I was an object of general affection and indulgence. I remember distinctly, and I see it now with my mind's eye, a cherry tree of fantastic shape that my cousin Persis, my contemporary, and I were in the habit of running up like kittens, to the dismay of my tender, sickly aunt, who would invariably raise her bedroom window and call out, "Girls, come down! you'll break your necks!" I am now the old crone!, and, alas I now should probably mar the sport of idle, fearless girls in the same way. No, dear Alice, I don't honestly think I should. I should be more like to *try* to climb the cherry tree with them!

When I lived at my uncle's, [it] was the period of the most bitter hostility between the Federalists and Democrats. The whole nation, from Maine to Georgia, was then divided into these two great parties. The Federalists stood upright, and with their feet firmly planted on the rock of Aristocracy, but that rock itself was bedded in sands, or rather was a boulder from the Old World, and the tide of democracy was surely and swiftly undermining it. The Federalists believed that all sound principles, truth, justice, and patriotism, were identified with the upper classes. They were sincere Republicans, but I think they began to fear a Republic could only continue to exist in Utopia. They were honest and noble men. The Democrats had among them much native sagacity; they believed in themselves, some from conceit, some from just conviction. They had less education, intellectual and moral, than their opponents, little refinement, intense desire to grasp the power and place that had been denied to them, and a determination to work out the theories of the government. All this, my dear Alice, as you may suppose, is an afterthought with me. Then I entered fully, and with the faith and ignorance of childhood, into the prejudices of the time. I thought every Democrat was grasping, dishonest, and vulgar, and would have in good faith adopted the creed of a staunch old parson, who, in a Fast-day sermon, said, "*I don't* say that every horse-thief is a Democrat, but I do say that every Democrat is a horse-thief!"

While I was at Bennington, I know not on what occasion to commemorate, small gold eagles were struck and presented to the ladies of conspicuous Federal families. My grownup cousins had them. They were sewn into the center of large bows they wore on their bonnets. I remember well pining in my secret soul that one was not given to me, and thinking that my father's position entitled me, though a child, to the distinction. One memorable Sunday, while my uncle was making the "long prayer," and I was standing on the bench in the clergyman's great square pew, my cousin Sally's bow got awry; the eagle "stooped" under its folds; and I, to save her from the ignominy of not showing her colors, walked around three sides of the pew, and disturbed not only my pious cousin's devotions, but many others, by the pother I made in rectifying the bow. I remember my good uncle, on being told of the exploit, instead of reproving me for my misdemeanor, heartily joined in the laugh.

After all, I believe there was a deal of good humor and village fun mingled in with the animosities. The village street, according to my recollection, extended a long way, some mile and a half, from a hill at one end to a plain at the other. There was a superannuated, particolored horse that had been turned off to find his own living by wayside grazing. He walked regularly from one end of the village placarded with attacks and rejoinders from the two parties and lampoons of all sorts. I have spoken of this in my tale—called I believe—Reminiscence of Federalism.[41]

My pleasant sojourn there was concluded by a bilious fever, through which I was tenderly attended by one of my cousins, a young physician. I suffered in my convalescence from the pangs of hunger, and one Sunday morning, having been left alone, and

[41]Sedgwick's childhood summer in Bennington, Vermont, served as the basis for "A Reminiscence of Federalism," which she published in *Tales and Sketches* (Philadelphia, 1835).

supposing all the family to be at church, I crept (I could not even stand alone) out of my bed, and down stairs to the buttery; but, on opening its door, there were two of my cousins regaling themselves with a lunch of cold chicken! I burst into tears at my discomfiture. They gave me a chicken-bone, and carried me back to my bed. The intense delight with which I gnawed that bone to its last fibre might enlighten the medical faculty.

I remember, while at Bennington, receiving from my father a morocco thread case and pocketbook, with a silver crown in it, and how enchanted I was. My father, generous without limit to his children, never would associate his comings home with gifts—he would have no craving but that of the affections. On one occasion, when I was a lisping child, some one asked me what papa brought me from Philadelphia. "Nothing," I replied, "but he called me his dear little lamb, his sweet little bird." This charmed my father and confirmed his theory.

My dear Alice, would you like to know what were the books of my childhood? You, of the present time, for whom the press daily turns out its novelties, for whom Miss Edgeworth has written her charming stories, and Scott has simplified history, will look upon my condition as absolute inanition.[42] The books that I remember (there were, perhaps, besides, a dozen little story-books) are Berquin's "Children's Friend," translated from the French, I think, in four volumes—I know I can remember the form and shade of color of the book, the green edges of the leaves, the look of my favorite

---

[42]Sedgwick's comments about the development of publishing in antebellum America were apt. The gross income derived from trade in books increased from $2,500,000 in 1820 to $12,500,000 three decades later. The Anglo-Irish author Maria Edgeworth (1767–1849) was extremely popular in this country. *Letters to Literary Ladies,* a defense of female education and Edgeworth's first publication, appeared in 1795; *Practical Education,* a similar volume, was issued three years later. Beginning with *Castle Rackrent,* published anonymously in 1800, Edgeworth's steady stream of novels brought her fame. In dedicating her first novel, *A New England Tale,* to Edgeworth, Sedgwick said that her inscription stood as a "slight expression of the writer's sense of her eminent service in the great cause of human virtue and improvement." Historical novels such as *Waverley, Rob Roy,* and *The Heart of Midlothian* made Sir Walter Scott famous on both sides of the Atlantic. The numerous references that Sedgwick herself made to Scott's novels suggest how familiar he was to readers in the United States.

pages.[43] Then there was the "Looking-glass," an eclectic, which contained that most pathetic story of "Little Jack."[44] Then there was a little thin book called "Economy of Human Life," made up of some small pieces of Mrs. Barbauld's.[45] That was quite above my comprehension, and I thought it very unmeaning and tedious. There was a volume of Rowe's "Letters from the Dead to the Living," which had a strange charm for me.[46] This was that charming poetry beginning "'Son of Mortality whence comest thou?'" I do not think that I believed them to have been actually written by the departed, but there was a little mystification about it that excited my imagination. And last and most delightful were the fables, tales, and ballads in a large volume of "Elegant Extracts."[47] I have sometimes questioned whether the keen relish which this scarcity of juvenile reading kept up, and the sound digestion it promoted, did not overbalance your advantage in the abundance and variety that certainly extinguishes some minds, and debilitates others with over-excitement.

From eight to eleven I remained at home—living according to my recollection a life of freedom and happiness—still no cloud over us but my dear mother's ill health. I went to the common school and to whatever "subscription school" there chanced to be in the

---

[43]A translation of Arnaud Berquin's *The Childrens Friend* appeared in 1783. Seventeen editions of the collected tales were available in English by 1800.

[44]*The Looking-Glass for the Mind; or Intellectual Mirror*, also by Arnaud Berquin, was published in 1787. The subtitle, *Being an Elegant Collection of the Most Delightful Little Stories and Interesting Tales*, suggests that these tales were also written for children. Twelve more editions of the volume were published in English by 1800.

[45]Anna Letitia Aikin Barbauld (1743–1825) published a series of miscellanies for children, none of which was issued under the title recalled by Sedgwick. Probably Sedgwick read either *Hymns in Prose for Children*, originally published in 1781, which appeared in 56 editions, or the equally popular *Lessons for Children* issued six years later.

[46]Elizabeth Singer Rowe's highly sentimental *Friendship in Death: In Twenty Letters from the Dead to the Living* was originally published in 1731. Thirty-one more editions had been published by 1800.

[47]Beginning in 1788, Vicesimus Knox, the editor of *Elegant Extracts*, published a series of volumes under this title. All contained excerpts from either prose or poetry. Sedgwick almost certainly read either *Elegant Extracts; or, Useful and Entertaining Passages in Prose, Selected for the Improvement of Young Persons* or its counterpart devoted to poetry, both of which were originally issued in 1790.

intervals of that. As I have before said my school life was a waste, my home life my only education.

I had two sisters. My eldest sister Eliza was married when I was seven and a half to Thaddeus Pomeroy. She had been mother and sister to me. She was of low stature, very dark complexion, soft brown eyes, profuse dark hair, and very regular and pretty features. Her form in her youth was symmetrical, and her hand and foot delicate and very pretty. I loved her dearly and I think her marriage gave me very early the impression that a wedding was rather a sundering than a forming of ties. Oh with what painful distinctness I remember the evening of the wedding. It was in the west front room in our old [home]. The family friends were gathered. In the middle of the ceremony while Doctor West was praying there suddenly came over me an awful sense of the reality of the separation that was consummating and I burst out into outcries of grief. When the prayer was closed, my father took me into his arms, he talked to me, he soothed me but all in vain, and finally I was carried into the east room. The servants came to bring me. "Kate," Mumbet whispered her "hush" but for the first time it was impotent. At last came the bridegroom and whispered "Your sister may stay with you this summer!" *May!* How my whole being revolted at the word. He had power to bind or loose my sister! There is an eloquent passage in one of Fanny Kemble's plays which she says was suggested by hearing me describe my feelings on this occasion.[48]

Oh dear sister what a life of trial, of patient endurance, of sweet hopes, heavenly affections, keen disappointments, harsh trials,

---

[48]The English actress and author Fanny Kemble (1809–1893) began her stage career at the age of 15, came to the United States three years later in 1832, and achieved national fame almost immediately. Following her marriage to Pierce Butler in 1834, Kemble left the stage for a decade. Her return, which coincided with the end of her marriage, combined acting with reading Shakespeare, a career that she pursued in both the United States and England. Kemble became a close friend of Sedgwick, her brother Charles, and his wife Elizabeth during the 1830s. After Kemble's divorce in 1849, she chose Lenox, Massachusetts, as her residence, in large part because of the proximity to Catharine, Charles, and Elizabeth. It is telling that Sedgwick repeated the anecdote about her sister's marriage. See p. 87. See the entry from Sedgwick's journal in which she describes her initial meeting with Kemble, p. 132.

acute sorrows and acute joys then opened upon you! What a life of truth, fidelity, faith, labor and love you lived. And just when you seemed to have come to a station of rest, when the children to whom you had so long been the mother-minister began to minister to you, you were stricken down! God's will be done. You have been saved many, many sorrows, and, I trust, see the purpose, unknown to us, of many afflictions that have since fallen on your house. Through my sister Eliza's life the tenderest union, the most unwavering confidence subsisted between us. A few days since I saw a letter from her in which she calls me her "sister—mother— child—friend."

She and my sister Frances were as unlike in character as in appearance. Frances was above the common stature with a fair skin and blooming cheeks that continued blooming all her life, hazel eyes, one of them particolored, beautiful bright chestnut hair, a roman nose, and a very handsome mouth. She was a great reader in her youth of poetry and romances. Eliza was occupied with household duties first in her father's house and then in her own—first nursing her mother and then supplying a mother's place to the children—and in her married life she had twelve children of her own to care for! Frances was excitable, irritable, enthusiastic, imaginative; Eliza calm, patient, reserved, sternly, scrupulously true. Frances was sympathetic and diffusive beyond any one I have ever known. Eliza's affections were within the range of her duties and strictly governed by them. No sphere could bound or contain Frances' interests or affections. Eliza was the steady light of her home; dear sister Frances shone widely and irregularly, but if ever a soul was kindled with holy fires hers was. She loved her friends with the faith and enthusiasm of devotees—but she sometimes changed her faith.

[Frances's] marriage was not a congenial one. She endured much heroically and [yet] through her sweet benevolence and wide sympathies she enjoyed a deal, though, to the superficial eye, her life seemed an utter failure. Never was any portion of it so complete a barren but she could find some flower to cherish, some fruit for refreshment. She never took a day drive in a stagecoach, or a night sail in a steamer but she found some wayfarer to whom she listened with faith and remembered with interest. She loved my father with passionate filial devotion, and all her family with enthusiastic affection. My sister Jane [Minot Sedgwick] loved her as if she were her own sister, and treated her with a mixture of filial and sisterly love that was *the* great blessing of my poor sister Frances's latter life. Your own Aunt Jane, Alice, who has been to each and all of us *our own.*[49]

Both my sisters were very religious. They were educated when the demonstration of religion and its offices made much more a part of life than now—when almost all of women's intellectual life took that tinge. They were both born with tendencies to the elevated and unseen; their religion was their pursuit, their daily responsibility, their aim, and end, and crowning affection.

They both began with the strict faith. Sister Eliza suffered from the horrors of Calvinism. She was so true, so practical, that she could not evade its realities; she believed its monstrous doctrines, and they made her gloomy; but for the last fifteen years of her life she was redeemed from this incubus; her faith softened into a true comprehension of the filial relation to God, and I have often heard her say that it was impossible for her to describe the happiness of her redemption from the cruel doctrines of Geneva.

Sister Frances's imagination saved her from a like suffering. However deep the slough into which she was cast, she would spread her wings and rise up into a pure atmosphere, bright with God's presence. She was one of those who believe without believing. Her faith was governed by her moods; when she was bilious and unhappy— very rarely—she sank down again into the slough. Thank God, their sweet spirits are now both expatiating in truth which is light.

My sisters were both married when I was still a child. I was but

---

[49]Jane Minot Sedgwick was married to Catharine's brother Harry. Jane and Harry moved to Stockbridge shortly after Harry's health began to fail in the 1820s, and she remained there after his death in 1831. I have deleted a paragraph in which Sedgwick

seven when my sister Eliza was married, and I remember that wedding evening as the first tragedy of my life.[50] She was my mothersister. I had always slept with her, and been her assigned charge. The wedding was in our "west room." I remember where the bride and her groom stood, and how he looked to me like some cruel usurper. I remember my father's place, and the rest is a confused impression of a room full of friends and servants—I think Mumbet stood by me. When the long consecrating prayer was half through, I distinctly remember the consciousness that my sister was going away from me struck me with the force of a blow, and I burst into loud sobs and crying. After the service, my father took me in his arms, and tried to quiet and soothe me, but I could be neither comforted nor quieted, so I stole out into the "east room," where Mumbet, Grippy, all the servants did their best to suggest consolations. Then came my new brother-in-law—how well I remember recoiling from him and hating him when he said to me, "I'll let your sister stay with you this summer." He let her! I was undressed and put into bed, and I cried myself to sleep and waked crying the next morning, and so, from that time to this, weddings in my family have been to me days of sadness, and yet, by some of them, I have gained treasures that no earthly balance or calculation can weigh or estimate! One of the finest passages in Fanny Kemble's "English Tragedy" was, as she told me, suggested by this passage between me and Dr. Pomeroy, which I had related to her.

My sister—dear faithful, humble, gentle Eliza—had I think rather a hard life of it—indifferent health and the painful drudgery of bearing and nurturing twelve children. Her husband was a man after the old pattern—resolute, fearless, enduring, generous, with alternations of tenderness and austerity, of impulsiveness and rigidity, that were trying to the gentle disposition and unvarying and

---

repeats the physical description of Eliza and Frances before she continues her narrative about their lives.

[50]As I have noted in the introduction, the fact that Sedgwick describes this incident twice underscores its impact upon her.

quiet devotion to duty of my sister. But her husband truly loved her and love truly covers a multitude of infirmities.

I remember well how dismal "Sister Eliza's" Albany life seemed to me. The contrast between the enjoyment and beauty and profusion of our own home and the crushing cares of her small tenement and necessarily narrow economies. Her religion during the Calvinistic ascendancy deepened the gloom. After about ten years residence in Albany Doctor P[omeroy's] health failed, he gave up business and to my parents' great delight came to live in Stockbridge, where now a single member of that large family lives in abundance of worldly goods, and in fearful famine of social sustenance—poor Mary![51] The first time my brother Charles made his sister a visit he was about six and seeing my sister paying her baker or milkman he came to my father and with tears in his eyes said, "Aren't you sorry for Sister Eliza. She has to pay money for her bread and her milk." No doubt he had believed these supplies came like sunshine and rain from Heaven. Susan Pomeroy was my friend, and beloved one of all my sisters' children. She was lost in the railroad tragedy at Norwalk in 1852.[52]

Three of my brothers were my seniors. I have no recollections of my eldest brother during my childhood. He was away at school and at college, but with my two brothers Harry and Robert I had intimate companionship, and I think as true and loving a friendship as ever existed between brothers and sister. Your "father Charles" was the youngest of the family, and so held that peculiar relation to us all as junior, and in some sort dependent, and the natural depository of our petting affections. I hardly know why, but I believe it was because my father could not bear to send him away from him, that his means of education were far inferior to his brothers'. He did not go to college, and, except a year or two's residence at Dr. Backus's, in Connecticut, I think he had no teaching beyond that of

[51]Born in 1815, Mary Pomeroy, the eleventh child of Thaddeus and Eliza Pomeroy, remained in Stockbridge until her death in 1872.

[52]Frances Susan Pomeroy, the seventh child of Thaddeus and Eliza Pomeroy, was born in 1807.

our common schools.[53] He had extreme modesty, and a habit of self-sacrifice and self-negation that I fear we all selfishly accepted. I do not think it ever occurred to him that he was quite equal to his brothers in mental gifts, and it was not till we had all got fairly into life that we recognized in him rare intellectual qualities. His heart was always to us the *image* of God.

Robert was my favorite brother. We were bound together from our childhood. I remember instances of tenderness while he was yet a little boy that are still bright as diamonds when so much has faded from my memory, or is dim to its eye.

But all my brothers were beloved, and I can conceive of no truer image of the purity and happiness of the equal loves of Heaven than that which unites brothers and sisters. It has been my chiefest blessing in life, and, but that I look to its continuance hereafter, I should indeed be wretched.

Your uncle Harry was, I think, intellectually superior to any of us. He had a wider horizon, more mental action, and I think he was the only one of us that had the elements of greatness. But he had great defects of mind, which, cooperating with the almost total loss of his eyesight, led to the great calamity of his life.[54] He had that absence of mind and fixity [of thought] so dangerous where the tendencies are all to what the Germans call subjectivity. Never was there a more loving, generous disposition than his, nor tenderer domestic affections.

(I have written these brief reminiscences at long intervals and now turning back the pages I see I have repeated the small events and observations of my life. I am fearful it will seem but a tedious croning of my dotage. But perhaps, if you, dear Alice, find so there

---

[53]The clergyman and educator Azel Backus (1765–1816) succeeded Joseph Bellamy as the minister of the Congregational Church in Bethlehem, Connecticut, in 1791. Backus's preparatory school, which he founded shortly after his arrival, attracted students throughout western New England.

[54]Harry Sedgwick suffered from mental illness during the last decade before his death in 1831. See the entries from Sedgwick's journal in which she describes the later years of her brother's life, pp. 116–118, 124, 129–131.

may be some among those of the generation before you who, when I am gone, will glance over it with interest.)

My first residence in New York the winter I was eleven was an era to me. I do not remember much of it. I have since heard from my sister Susan [Ridley Sedgwick] that she too was sent from her country home to spend the winter there.[55] She says she too went to the dancing school of Monsieur Lalliet and felt very forlorn. She stayed at Brockholst Livingston's, her uncle, and had for her only acquaintance her cousin Susan L. (since Mrs. Ledyard), then a wild, ungoverned, tyrannical child.[56] Susan says she saw a little girl with bright yellow hair hanging in curls over her face and neck towards whom she felt drawn, as seeming to have something to answer to her wants. She too was a stranger among the girls, and she tried in vain to ascertain her name til one day she dropped her pocket handkerchief and picking it up she found the name Catharine M. Sedgwick worked in hair upon it (no indelible ink in those days). But those two girls passed away from M. Lalliet's unknown to each other and never dreamed of the relation that was to bond them through life in most true friendship! It was Theodore that introduced me at that school—but no magnetic impulse disclosed to him his future wife![57]

I first went to the theatre that winter—an epoch in a child's life. It was in the time of the Hodgkinsons, charming performers, and

---

[55]Susan Ridley married Theodore Sedgwick in 1808. Except for a brief period in which Charles Sedgwick occupied the family's homestead in Stockbridge, Susan and Theodore lived there throughout their marriage, and Susan continued to reside there after Theodore's death in 1839. Although not as well known as her sister-in-law Catharine, Susan Ridley Sedgwick also had a long literary career. In 1829, she published *The Morals of Pleasure: Illustrated by Stories Designed for Young Persons.* Her other titles included *Allen Prescott: or, the Fortunes of a New England Boy* (1834), *Alida; or, Town and Country* (1844), and *Walter Thornley; or, A Peep at the Past* (1859).

[56]Beginning in 1806, Henry Brockholst Livingston (1757–1823) served as a justice on the United States Supreme Court for 17 years. Prior to this appointment, he was a judge on New York's Supreme Court. "Susan L." who was Livingston's daughter, married Benjamin Ledyard.

[57]In a fragment tucked inside the cover of vol. I of the autobiography, Sedgwick constructed an alternative portrayal of her initial meeting with Susan Ridley Sedgwick. I have inserted the paragraph on pp. 93–94.

in the beginning of Cooper's career.[58] He was the first of second-rate tragedians. My first play was Macbeth. Hodgkinson played Macbeth, Cooper Macduff. When they came to the final fight, I entreated my brother to take me out of the house. He laughed at me. I said, "I know it is not real, but they are really enraged!" How much delight I had from the few plays I saw that winter. What an exquisite portion of the pleasures of imagination come or have come to the young through the drama. To this day, the drying at the fire of a wet newspaper recalls the eagerness with which I dried the daily paper to read the play-bill, and truly it is now a sweet odor to me!

The events of the winter were the birth of my sister [Frances's] eldest child, Theodore, and a visit from my dear father and brother Robert. Robert even then made great fun of the wardrobe in which he had been sent to the city by our frugal Aunt Anne who was the administrator at home. He has often since recalled it and described it, and it may be put in picturesque contrast to the Paris dress of his grandson (the little God) or it might illustrate the progress of usury since that day. The son of a humble merchant would not now run down to New York so rustically equipped. He had one pair of pantaloons home-spun and home-dyed—butternut colored—the color he declared came off if you looked at them and another "best pair" made from a fine old cashmere coat of his older brothers and which he said cracked whenever he moved. Luckily for his toilette he had the measles during his visit and no occasion for dress. He amused himself with my fine lady airs and said the butternut pants must petrify me, that when he was walking out with me I espied some dancing school acquaintance and turned Levite upon him![59]

---

[58]Shortly after his arrival in the United States, the English actor John Hodgkinson (1767–1805) became a familiar figure on the stage. Hodgkinson's versatility made him representative of his generation. His fellow Englishman Thomas Abthorpe Cooper (1776–1849) became one of America's most popular actors.

[59]Turning the Levite derives from the story of the good Samaritan. Unlike the Samaritan who helped the man that had been robbed and beaten on the road from Jerusalem to Jericho, the Levite "looked on him, and passed on the other side." See Luke 10:32.

I did not at that period form any girlish friendships or any acquaintance out of my dancing school. There was an old lady who lived opposite to my sister whom I was very fond of visiting and to this day I recall her kindly aspect, her florid complexion, her pots of beautiful astemesias, and her pleasant tales about the Revolution in which, I believe, her husband had played a conspicuous part as Commissary. How well I remember those flowers, flowers I have always loved next to *dear* living creatures, and I can recall the look and odor of the particular friends of my early childhood—the damask and cinnamon roses under our front porch windows and in the garden, the large plant of old fashioned honest peonies that stood near the little garden gate, the blue bells, and above all the *pinks*, my mother's favorite and till now the memorial I wear through all the summer months for her.

I read constantly, but chiefly novels. I remember little of that winter, but falling romantically in love with a handsome young man, the half brother of Mr. Watson, who had just returned from abroad. It was the fancy of a few weeks of a girl of eleven! I knew him afterwards, a cold selfish but still handsome man.

I went once to a large family dinner at Jacob Morton's with my brother Theodore. Our host asked me, the only stranger, which part of a huge turkey in which he had put his carving fork I would take. I knew only one point of manners for such occasions, dear Alice, that I must specify some part and as ill luck would have it, the side bone came first into my head and "side bone, sir," I said. Oh what a lecture I got [when we got home]—the wretched "little chit that compelled a gentleman to cut up a whole turkey to serve her." I cried myself to sleep that night. My brother, then a student at law in Mr. Riggs' office, was very ambitious that his sister should be an adept in the polite arts. From that time till I was sixteen or seventeen I had an inexpressible dread of his observation and criticism. My manners were frank, confiding, and artless but not conventional. And neither my brother nor my long social life has taught me to be so.

The last recollection I have of New York is of spending my last five dollars in a greenhouse for plants which I brought home with me! And here I must tell you a piece of boyish, practical, cruel fun of my brother Robert. He pulled up all my precious *costly* plants and in the place of my Meander, holy anthus, geraniums, etc., he put down milkweed, mullin, catnip and all plebian things and appended to these long Latin names.

It was at this early period of our lives that your Aunt Susan and I first met.[60] Could it have been foreseen by any cast of our horoscopes how lovingly our destinies were to mingle? In that pleasant dancing-room in Broad Street we two country girls met. She had been sent to her Uncle Brockholst Livingston, then an eminent judge in the United States [Supreme] Court, to be perfected in the arts and graces of young ladies. Her rare intelligence had been developed by rare opportunities. She had led a romantic life for three or four years on our frontier, living partly in a fort with General [William Henry] Harrison, afterwards President of the United States. She had that rare gift refinement cultivated by high breeding and she revolted from the rantipole manners of the undisciplined crew of girls headed by her proud, undisciplined, lawless cousin Susan Livingston (Mrs. Ledyard). Susan Ridley was a little my senior. She remembered noticing a quiet little girl, whose behavior was rather a contrast to the rabble rout. She was she said interested by her demeanor, her face, and her abundant curling hair. She longed for her companionship. She did not even know her name till one day she picked up a pocket handkerchief the girl dropped and she found marked on it with hair (the fashion that preceeded the introduction of indelible ink) C. M. *Sedgwick*. The name she was to hear and enrich and transmit. But we were yet to remain strangers. My less fastidious sympathies soon bound me up with the romping girls and my future sister remained apart.

---

[60]This recollection of Susan Ridley Sedgwick is part of the fragment that was left inside the back cover of vol. I. Because Sedgwick's visit to New York City is the subject of the immediately preceeding paragraphs and the fragment itself, the description of Sedgwick's initial encounter with the young Susan Ridley has been inserted here. See the alternative version on p. 90.

About three years after we met at Mrs. Bell's boarding school at Albany. She was just finishing a term of two years when I entered the school as a day scholar. I remained at the noon recess and a beautiful girl, Angelica Gilbert, afterwards a belle of New York, with a sweet and graceful courtesy that made a lasting impression on me, offered to teach me (an unknown art to me then) ropejumping. And when I was fairly inducted and going home one of the mannerless girls shouted out to me, "Give Miss Ridley's love to your brother!" I turned and saw a delicate, fair, elegant girl overpowered with confusion blushing up to the roots of her soft brown hair who cried out to me, "O, don't—don't." In fact, some months before this time a mutual interest between her and my brother Theodore had begun which continued through their most happy marriage with a purity, strength, and mutual confidence and joint blessing to others that might authorize and confirm the belief that "marriages are made in Heaven."

31 August 1854. Another year is gone, and I am admonished that few *can* remain to me, and this day, at 12 a. m., alone in my little parlor, your dear father and mother [William and Kate Sedgwick Minot] here [in Lenox] on their annual visit, (gone off to Otis on a recuperative excursion!) having just finished telling a fairy tale to you, and Will, and Lucy Pike. I have taken my pen to note some changes in the condition of our village since I was young. I remember the making of the turnpike through Stockbridge—I think it must have been about forty years ago—and that was a great era then for it enabled us to have a stagecoach three days in the week from Boston to Albany, and three from Albany to Boston. In due time came the daily coach, arriving, after driving the greater part of two nights, the middle of the second day from Boston.

It then seemed there could be nothing in advance of this. Your [great] uncle Theodore has the honor of being the first person who conceived the possibility of a railroad over the mountains to Connecticut River. He proposed it in the [Massachusetts] Legislature, and argued so earnestly for it, that it became a very common reproach to him that he was crazy.[61] Basil Hall, when he was in Stock-bridge, ridiculed the idea, and said to your [great] uncle, "If you had it, what would you carry over it?"[62] He did not live to be con-futed, nor your [great] uncle to witness the triumph of his opinion, but I have lived this very summer to travel to the Mississippi by rail! The daily coach was a great advance on my earliest experience, when a mongrel vehicle, half wagon, half coach, drawn by horses that seemed to me like Time to the Lover, came once a week from New York, letting the light from the outer world into our little val-ley, and bringing us letters from "Papa." Now, at 3 P.M., we read the paper issued the same morning at New York.

We had one clergyman in Stockbridge, of sound New England orthodoxy, a Hopkinsian Calvinist. Heaven forbid, dear Alice, that you should ever inquire into the splitting of these theological hairs. Sixty years he preached to us, and in all that time, though there may have been at some obscure dwelling a Methodist or Baptist ranter, the "pious" of the town all stood by the Doric faith. The law then required each town to support a clergyman, and his salary was paid by taxation. The conscience was left free. He who preferred to dis-sent from the prevailing religion could on assigning his reasons "sign off," but I believe he was required to transfer his allegiance to some other ministry. Now the clergy are supported by the voluntary system, and a man may revert to heathenism (and some do!) and no man call him to account. I have elsewhere and repeatedly de-scribed our good pastor of sixty years—stern as an old Israelite in his faith, gentle and kindly in his life as my Uncle Toby. I dreaded

---

[61]In 1827, Theodore Sedgwick presented a bill to the Masachusetts legislature that provided for the construction of a railroad between Boston and Albany. Its route in-cluded Stockbridge. Initially, the idea met with relatively little support. But two decades later, the Stockbridge and Pittsfield Railroad was chartered and the first train arrived in Stockbridge on Jan. 1, 1850.

[62] After a visit to the United States in 1827 and 1828, the British naval officer Basil Hall published his controversial *Travels in North America*, a three-volume criticism of antebellum democracy. Hall's negative commentary notwithstanding, he did praise Catharine Sedgwick, describing her novels as "admirable works of fancy." He was im-pressed as well with "the graphic truth with which the country in which the scenes are laid is described" (p. 74).

him and certainly did not understand him in my youth. He was then only the dry, sapless embodiment of polemical divinity. It was in my mature age and his old age that I discovered his Christian features, and found his unsophisticated nature as pure and gentle as a good little child's. He stood up in the pulpit for sixty years and logically proved the whole moral creation of God (for this he thought limited to earth, and the stars made to adorn man's firmament) left by him to suffer eternally for Adam's transgression, except a handful *elected* to salvation, and yet no scape-grace, no desperate wretch within his ken died without some hope for his eternal state springing up in the little doctor's merciful heart. Some contrite word, some faint aspiration, a last slight expression of faith on the deathbed, a motion, a look, were enough to save this kind heart from despair of any fellow creature.

Dr. [Stephen] West belonged to other times than ours. His three cornered beaver, and Henry Ward Beecher's Cavalier hat, fitly denote the past and present clerical dynasties, the first formal, elaborate, fixed, the last easy, comfortable, flexible, and assuming nothing superior to the mass.[63] I did not love him nor yet fear him while I was a child. I saw him in friendly interaction with my parents and besides (Here ended that writing and now November 12, 1854, I am resuming it). I will try to sketch the doctor's outward man for you. He was not, I think, above five feet in height. His person was remarkably well made and erect, and I think the good little polemic was slightly vain of it, for I remember his garments fitted accurately, and nice hose (in summer always of black silk) displayed a handsome calf and ankle, and his shining black shoes and silver buckles impressed even my careless eye. He had good teeth (then a rare beauty) even to his oldest age, but all his features were graceless, and there was nothing approaching comeliness of form or expression, but an eye ever ready to flow with gentle pity and tender sym-

---

[63]Henry Ward Beecher (1813–1887) was late 19th-century America's most prominent evangelical minister. Having abandoned the Calvinism of his father, Lyman Beecher, Henry Ward embraced a theology of universal salvation. The contrast between him and West could not have been more stark.

pathy. His hair was cut à la Cromwell, as if a bowl had been inverted on his head, and his foretop cut by its rim. And he had always a little comb in his pocket. His knock at the "east door" was as recognizable as his voice. That opened to him, he came in, and, taking off his hat, saluted each member of the family, down to the youngest, with the exact ceremony and something of the grace of a French courtier. He then walked up to the table between the two front windows, deposited the three-cornered beaver, put his gloves in his hat, and his silver-headed cane in the corner, and then, taking [a] little comb from his pocket, he smoothed down his thin locks, so that every numbered hair on his head lay in its appointed place. Then the dear little gentleman sat down and compressed the geniality of his nature into the social hour that followed, being, during that hour, uniformly served with the fitting type of that geniality— a good glass of wine. These visits occurred always once a week; and, if any temporalities in the church occured requiring confidence or consultation, as much oftener as he felt the want of my father's sympathy or advice, for it was rather noticeable that, for these purposes, he preferred my father to any or all of the "elect."

Poor old gentleman. His last days were not his best days. He had a colleague who was a sneaking fellow frequenting men and women gossips, and fabricating scandal against the little doctor and his second helpmeet, and endeavoring thereby to monopolize to himself the favor of the parish and the whole salary.[64] The doctor's age had imposed seclusion. He was personally almost a stranger to the generation just grown, and suddenly it was discovered that the greater part of his people were alienated from him, and that many believed that he and his wife lived in a drunken companionship. Those who knew the almost Judaical regularity and strictness of his life, and the truth of hers, earnestly adhered to them. Council after council

[64]In 1810, Ephraim Swift, a graduate of Williams College, joined the elderly West. The two shared West's ministry until Swift tried to destroy their parishioners' confidence in his colleague and have him removed. As Sedgwick notes in her description of the controversy, West emerged with his reputation intact, although in the interests of restoring harmony to the community he agreed to be dismissed. Swift was forced to resign.

was called, the town was divided into factions. Mrs. West, a feeble, trembling, timid old lady, was barbarously put upon trial, as cruel as the "putting to the question" and no satisfactory evidence appeared against her. Then the doctor's life and habits were put to proof. After ruinous hearsays were detailed, [and] rags of gossip, that had been manufactured by the colleague [Ephraim] Swift and passed from hand to hand, were disposed of, Parson Kinne was called up.[65] He was an old polemic, a man of staunch honesty whose truth no man believed could be shaken. He had resided in Dr. West's family six months at a time. He had been so scrupulously reserved that no one knew what he would testify. The Swifts believed it would be full-out against the doctor, and we, his friends, shivered lest the good old man might have been perverted from a right judgment by the crafty communications and insinuations of Swift, and might have misinterpreted the doctor's habit of taking a single cheerful glass during the day. Kinne was as grotesque in looks and manners as Dominie Sampson, and to some of us it seemed that Scott must have been gifted with second sight, and drawn "little Harry's" tutor after the pattern of our Puritan.[66] I shall never forget when he was called on and stood up within the semicircle— an awful halo—of clergymen around him. He said that, during a ride with Mr. Swift two or three years before, that gentleman had told him that Dr. West and lady were guilty of gross drinking—that they consumed such an amount of rum (specifying it) in a month—that the doctor set a mug of rum by his bedside at night and rose repeatedly to drink it—etc., etc., etc. And all this while Mr. Kinne was living in the family. "Did you believe this, sir?" asked one of the council. The old man shook his faded yellowish wig, smiled with a most comical mixture of contempt, triumph, and simplicity, and replied, "Not—one—word—of—it—sir!" A low murmur of shame and disappointment ran over the assembly, while

[65]Congregational clergyman Aaron Kinne (1744–1824) was Stephen West's counterpart in nearby Egremont, Massachusetts.

[66]Tutor to Henry Bertram in *Guy Mannering*, Walter Scott's Domine Sampson displayed a striking "awkwardness of manners and simplicity of character."

a sort of feu de joie [bonfire] broke from the few devoted friends and allies of the good old man.

Mean, vulgar, cruel as the persecution was, it never touched within the holy circle of the doctor's charities, never invaded his peace, nor clouded his serenity. He even, through the whole of Swift's crawling through his slimy way, "hoped that now, Mr. Swift meant to do better" and not one bitter word or shadow of resentment escaped him, so that after sixty years of utterly useless polemical preaching, he closed his career with "practical observations" on love, charity, forgiveness, and self-negation, that sunk deep in some of our hearts.

I remember one anecdote rather illustrative of his preaching. He held the Hopkinsian doctrine that Christ died to manifest God's wrath against sin, repudiating the strictly Calvinistic doctrine of Christ's vicarious atonement. Upon one occasion, Dr. [John Mitchell] Mason, of New York, who then was the most conspicuous pulpit orator in the country—a man confident in his faith and bold to audacity—preached for Dr. West.[67] Mason was a tall, burly, fair man, in the heart and vigor of life. I cannot forget the figures of the two men, as they stood together, for our pastor was perfect in the ceremonials of courtesy, which he would not violate by sitting down in his own pulpit. Dr. M. thundered away in a sermon of an hour and a half upon the doctrine of substitution, every eye fixed on him in the deepest attention. The next day the "little Doctor" (so my father always styled him) came as usual, and, in talking over the sermon he said, "The people did not understand one word that he said," and then added with a sigh, and oh! with what mournful truth, "and I am afraid they have never understood me either."

Nearly seven years after she began her autobiography, Sedgwick returned to it in the spring of 1860. She was now seventy. Numbering

[67]Clergyman John Mitchell Mason (1770-1829) upheld Calvinist doctrine during a long career in which he ministered to a prominent congregation in New York City, served as the provost at Columbia College, and held the presidency of Dickinson College. Those who heard Mason generally agreed with Sedgwick's evaluation.

only eighteen pages in manuscript, the second volume is replete with the two worlds in which Sedgwick resided during the final years of her life. Described as representative of a "double consciousness," the first of these worlds was inhabited by the dead, the second and ostensibly less satisfying by the living. With the death of her brother Charles in 1856, Catharine became the only surviving member of her generation. Her thought that spring of 1860 that "I alone am left" was made more salient by the deaths of Eliza Cabot Follen and Anna Jameson, both friends of long standing who like Sedgwick had pursued literary careers. In this volume of her recollections, Sedgwick brought together two main forms of autobiographical writing, the autobiography and the journal. On one page she recalled the days she had spent as a student at Mrs. Bell's in Albany nearly six decades earlier, on another a lecture by John Weiss that she had heard the day before, on still another the books she had read the previous winter. Inadvertently, then, Sedgwick herself provided the transition to the selections from the journals that follow the autobiography.

March 10, 1860. At the latest period of my life I am retracing the earliest. The dear home was then *alive.* All the loving forms that made it so have long passed away, the loving voices are silent. I alone am left. These last words are the keynote to multitudinous recollections—*recollections!* Those who have passed away to others' senses are present to mine, present always to those subtle and spiritual senses behind the grosser bodily organs. I have a double consciousness—a world within the world of beings whose experience, thought, feelings flow in the same current with mine and then [there] are those living about me now running a stream parallel to mine but having a distinct life. I partake in the sunshine and the clouds that fall on them. Some among them are my happiness, my consolation, the balm, the marrow of my present life. Still I am alone, a lingerer behind all that came with me to the work of life.

My present life does not satisfy me. I am doing nothing. With health and faculties still capable I am idle. There are no results to my days. The ground that I once tilled lies fallow. I go to see my friends, and their affections and sympathies make my presence an enjoyment to them. And I can at least credit myself with the desire and effort to make it so. But this is but a barren service for these last few days of sunshine. I came to Woodbourne on the twenty-third of December.[68] I have been uniformly well—and except for the death of my precious friend Eliza Follen[69] there has been nothing in my outer world to disturb its serenity, much to awaken gratitude and fortify trust. Two more children have been born with my brother Charles's blood in their veins. God grant them with that same portion of that spirit that made his life a blessing to his sphere, a joy and thankfulness to me.

I went yesterday for the third time to hear Mr. [John] Weiss in his course of lectures on the Greeks. He told us of the German [Friedrich August] Wolf who in the interval between the American and French Revolutions denied the authenticity of Homer's poems on the ground of want of unity, and from the impossibility of one mind retaining and reciting a continuous poem of the length of the Iliad, and from the want of occasions among the Greeks for the recitation of a poem of such length.[70] These criticisms have, I suppose, long been dispersed in empty air. To us unlearned ladies Mr. W. answered the German by a very ingenious development of the plot of the Iliad showing that the unities had been duly respected

---

[68]Woodbourne, the home of Sedgwick's niece Kate Sedgwick Minot and her family, was located in West Roxbury, Massachusetts.

[69]Author and abolitionist Eliza Lee Cabot Follen (1787–1860) was one of Sedgwick's intimate friends. Sedgwick introduced her to Charles Follen, a political refugee from Germany, whom Cabot married in 1828. Together they became deeply involved in abolitionism. In addition to antislavery tracts, Follen had an extremely varied literary career during which she compiled *Selections from the Writings of Fenelon*, issued a fictional homily concerning matrimonial happiness, edited a juvenile magazine, and published volumes of children's stories.

[70]German classical scholar Friedrich August Wolf (1759–1824) suggested that the *Iliad* and the *Odyssey* inherited from the classical world might have been composed by several authors. Initially, Wolf's controversial theory as presented in *Prolegomena ad Homerum* (1795) held sway. But by the middle of the 19th century when Sedgwick attended the series of lectures other scholars had begun to challenge Wolf. Nonetheless, Wolf is credited with transforming the study of Homer and introducing the approaches that characterize modern philology.

by the Father of Poetry.[71] That after opening with the wrath of Achilles and cause of it and Achilles withdrawal he had permitted the Greeks through five books to be victorious without him only to show that at the culminating point of the conflict, when they had been driven back and thoroughly beaten by Hector, Achilles, who had resisted the offer of his Brisaius, of cities, of fame, renown and all costly gifts, came forward to revenge Patroclus's death and finally in complete triumph dragged Hector's body twelve times around the walls of Troy. He said not only had the Ancients recited the whole but learned Germans and Oxford scholars [had done the same]. He classed Homer with Shakespeare and Milton and assigned him the first place. This no merely English scholar will assent to, the assertion though may seem to him monstrous. He quoted two passsages which he called Shakespearian, and they were tinged with his high quality. And so you might find exquisite specimens of trees and flowers and singing birds in a gentleman's grounds, but for that are they equal to *all* the world without them?

He spoke of the exquisite humor of the mythology. It may be so, but to a mere reader of Pope's Homer[72] there seems not to be so much of that sunshine humor as may be found in one of Sydney Smith's or even dear Charles Lamb's Essays[73]—not so much as in one playful half hour of my brother Charles's life at his fireside.[74]

The two memorable books of this winter, the sensation books,

---

[71]The Unitarian minister John Weiss (1818–1879) was almost certainly the lecturer to whom Sedgwick referred. He lectured widely on Greek literature and also helped to introduce Americans to German authors such as Schiller and Goethe.

[72]"Pope's Homer," as it was commonly called, refers to Alexander Pope's six-volume translation of Homer's *Iliad*, published between 1715 and 1720. The translation was popular in both England and the United States throughout the 18th and early 19th centuries.

[73]Poet, playwright, and essayist Charles Lamb (1775–1834) published collections of essays, many of which concerned literature. The initial volume of essays, which appeared in 1818, was followed by collections in 1823 and 1833.

[74]The essayist Sydney Smith (1771–1845), one of the founders of the widely read *Edinburgh Review*, contributed more than 80 articles in the first three decades of the 19th century. Many of these were collected in his *Works*, issued in four volumes in 1839 and 1840. Smith's famous wit was nowhere more pointed than in the query he published in the *Review* in 1820. "In the four quarters of the globe," he asked rhetorically, "who reads an American book? or goes to an American play? or looks at an American picture

are Florence Nightingale's Notes on Nursing and Hawthorne's Marble Faun.[75] It is not the depoetised utilitarian alone that will pronounce the first the greatest work, informed as it is by the genius of Love, a far more blessed potency than the genius of Intellect. Miss Nightingale comprehends the material world of nursing and gives certain directions in relation to it in the clearest, most direct, most intelligible way, so that one can scarcely be so blundering or so weak as not to learn from her how to apply her instructions. And further than this with senses *subtleised* by compassion and tenderness she sees and hears the disturbances of the spirit (which in a diseased body is jangled and out of tune) imperceptible and inaudible to common observers.

Hawthorne by the gorgeous light with which he is endowed lights us through Italy. He shows to our minds eye what never of its own power it could see, and he lights up the dim chambers of memory, illuming our faded impressions, putting his own glowing colors on them, and often a thrilling interpretation on what to common senses are but blank walls. But it seems to me his story mars his book. It reminds me of a peep into Bluebeard's chamber at the theater in my childhood, a glimpse of unintelligible horror. It is a cruel

---

or statue?" Sedgwick's appreciation of Smith notwithstanding, she would have found this statement gratuitous.

[75]Published in 1860, Florence Nightingale's *Notes on Nursing: What It Is And What It Is Not* called for professional training in nursing. She insisted that nursing's practitioners be educated in the scientific basis of medicine and that nursing itself be considered a profession. Nightingale also displayed the compassion to which Sedgwick referred. Telling nurses that they must empathize with the ill, she called upon them to acknowledge that the patient "is face to face with his enemy all the time, internally wrestling with him, having long imaginary conversations with him." The patient's paramount concern, she added, is elimination "of his adversary quickly." These tenets shaped the education offered at the Nightingale Training School for Nurses, which was founded the same year as *Notes on Nursing* was published. *The Marble Faun, or the Romance of Monte Beni*, the novel that Sedgwick found so disturbing, is a study in the consequences of human sin. The lives of the heroine Miriam and her Italian suitor, Donatello, are destroyed by the murder of a mysterious figure who stalks Miriam. Donatello, a simple and entirely innocent character at the beginning of the novel, kills Miriam's persecuter. Miriam herself is complicit in the act. His sense of guilt awakened, Donatello is imprisoned for his crime. An ostensibly free Miriam is shackled by the grief that is generated by her involvement in the murder.

endowment of the children of his imagination. (Here I was inter-rupted and I have lost the idea).

7 April [1860] I have been reading a portion of Kingsley's late edition of the "Fool of Quality," a book I remember as among my father's loves—one of the few novels in our old library at Stock-bridge.[76] How well do I remember the five duodecimo volumes, in their dark leather bindings. The favorite books of that time stand around the chambers of memory, each a shrine. In this there is much wit and pathos, nature and wisdom (nature *is* wisdom when it is evolved from the human heart and from life). The style seems to me admirable, something in the fashion of the quaint old coats of our grandfathers, fashioned for ease and use, and of the best broadcloth garnished with velvet.

It seems to me an admirable book might be made out of it for children, and I have a great mind to try my hand at it. It might, perhaps, flatter a little too much the dynasties of the present day, the young usurpers of their fathers' thrones.

April 7 1860 (!) I believe no school days were as to systematic school learning less productive than mine. Till I was twelve I had had no school instruction except at the common school of the vil-lage, unless indeed my nibble at French should be excepted. At twelve I was sent to Mrs. Bell's school in Albany. This school had enjoyed great reputation and was sustained by the first families in the land. Mrs. Bell was a decayed gentlewoman, of Irish descent (indeed, I rather think born in Ireland). She had been much in the society of clever men, had a very cheerful disposition, and various social talents. But alas I had already too much social taste and facil-ity, and the bane of my life—a want of order and system—found no antidote there. Mrs. Bell was a serious invalid, and had become a regular valetudinarian in all her habits. She rose late, was half the

---

[76]Written by the playwright and novelist Henry Brooke, *The Fool of Quality, or, The History of Henry, Earl of Moreland* was published in five volumes between 1766 and 1770. The two-volume edition of the novel to which Sedgwick referred was issued with a biographical preface by Charles Kingsley in 1819. In describing its moral and spiritual power, Kingsley, an Anglican prelate, ranked the novel with Spenser's *Faerie Queen.*

time out of her school, and did very little when in it. But she was always ready to throw out poetic riddles and conundrums that charmed us, and all the more that they generally involved some little love-preference or romantic incident of the school-girls. She had decided leanings towards those pupils who were cleverest and socially most attractive and connected with her friends out of school bounds. She liked to have us with her in the evening, and to attract to her circle the intelligent people within her reach.

At Mrs. Bell's I again met my brother Theodore's future wife Susan Ridley. She was about eighteen months older than I. She had been three years at the school and was about leaving it, a full grown, very elegant, and according to the standard of those times a very accomplished young woman. My Brother introduced me at the school. I was received by Miss Baxter, the niece and assistant of Mrs. Bell. She received me with a practiced, easy air, and a sweeping curtesy that daunted the poor little rustic. It was the peacock spreading his tail before a poor little straggler from the coop. And when my brother afterward reproved my "little dot of a curtesy," I was ready to sink into the ground.

I was but a day-scholar and when I was tying on my hat at noon to go home, Miss Angelica Gilbert, the most beautiful girl of her day, called me to where she stood encircled by school-girls and said, "give Miss Ridley's love to your brother." "O, no—no—don't—don't," exclaimed a voice and turning I saw a tall, fair, elegant girl, her face suffused and her lips trembling.[77] My future sister. My dear friend from that hour without variableness or shadow of turning, I may say without irreverence, for she has intensely struggled to conform to the admonition, "be ye perfect as your Father in Heaven is perfect" and has succeeded as far as human infirmity admits.

Her schoolmate had divined her feelings, for even then in the very dawn of her womanhood she gave her heart to my brother. Through all her young lady days she was admired and followed, and

[77]Sedgwick also described this incident in the autobiographical fragment that was tucked inside the back cover of vol. I. The fragment has been inserted in the text. See p. 94.

for two gay winters in New York and Boston [she was] a cynosure in the fashionable world. But she was unwavering in her love for the young Albany lawyer and though uncertain as to his love for her she kept the treasure of her heart till he touched its spring.

She was naturally drawn to me. I can take little credit for this. I loved her enthusiastically, and never, I am sure, desired any good for myself more earnestly than her hand for my brother. She remained but a short time at school, but even then we began a correspondence which has continued to this time. We had a mailbag hanging in the school, which was each day filled and discharged. Of course, as you may suppose, dear Alice, I was a large contributor to this daily literature.

There was another gifted girl at the school, Mary North. She became a *lover* of mine, and was jealous of every school girl that I liked. She had been much flattered by her elders, she was conscious of superiority, and thought the first place was her right. To me she was affectionate and true. She was handsome too, which is not reckoned a secondary gift to a woman. She disappointed expectation by her early death. I think she was not more than seventeen when she died. I have retained to this day an affectionate and grateful recollection of her—grateful, because she once honestly and kindly told me of a besetting infirmity of mine, and made me earnestly desire to eradicate it. It is not her fault that I have not. You will see, my dear Alice, that I had, if not the legitimate means of instruction, at least some rare advantages in my school days—the elevating society and friendship of a superior woman and cultivated companions and friends who enriched my mind, though it was not laid out, planted, and tilled quite in the right way.

I learned a few days since, by an obituary written by [William Cullen] Bryant, [of] the death of Mrs. [Anna] Jameson.[78] She was

[78]Sedgwick pasted a fragment of the obituary to the inside of the front cover of vol. II. The British author Anna Jameson (1794–1860) wrote widely on topics ranging from Shakespeare's heroines to Christian iconography. A strong supporter of women's rights, she insisted that both sexes were "*equally* rational beings with improvable faculties, *equally free*, to choose the good and refuse the evil, equally destined to an equal immor-

among the few friends of my happiest years left to me. She came to
this country in 1837 with the purpose of reunion to her husband
and at his invitation. She went to Toronto (in Canada) and was
dishonestly treated, being received with all proper observance before spectators, and met with entire and disdainful silence when
they were alone. To preside in her husband's house in this relation
to him with contentment and unsuspected satisfaction was impossible, and after a few weeks she returned to New York and embarked
for England, where her presence was essential to the happiness of
her family and her exertions to their support. The cause of her conjugal disappointment is not to be told. It reflected no dishonor or
question upon her but deep disgrace on her husband. Mr. John
Duer, her able lawyer, believed he invited her here to escape a contract to pay her annually $1,500, a pitiful stipend from a salary of
$20,000, the income of an office which she had obtained for him!
The contract was annulled by her return to his roof. But Mr. Duer's
obtained a renewal of it. I believe [he did so] by making the man
realize the meanness and deep disgrace of his conduct. Mrs. Jameson came to Stockbridge to see me before I had seen her. She was
kindly received by my friends (as who was not?) but I think not
with the enthusiasm she might have expected from her celebrity.
She came to your Aunt Jane's and to your "Father Charles." Your
Aunt Jane was rather jealous of the widening circle of my acquaintance which took me so much from my family, and she always
recoiled from "public characters," and your "Father Charles"
could not endure conventional restraints upon social intercourse.
It was indeed like turning a mountain brook into a canal channel
and fettering its free leaps and innocent overflowings by dams
and embankments. But Mrs. Jameson was essentially a free, impulsive woman. She was Irish, and an Irish strata underlaid her
whole character. She remained several days at Lenox, told charm-

tality." Jameson also suggested that *The Englishwoman's Journal* be established, supported younger reformers such as Barbara Bodichon, and became a founding member
of the Society for the Promotion of Employment of Women. See the entry from Sedgwick's journal on their friendship, p. 154.

ing stories to your mother and her brother. Charles sung joyously Irish songs and sung also plaintive English ballads. She perceived the exquisite texture of my brother's character and thoroughly enjoyed his humor as pure sparkling and perennial as if it were indeed (selon [according to] Mr. Weiss) the element of Homer's gods.

Mrs. Jameson repeatedly expressed to me a feeling of gratitude. She would say, "you do not know how grateful I am to you, nor why." I did not feel at liberty to ask her what she did not tell without asking. I had done *nothing* towards her, and I could only infer that some chance seed in my writing might have fallen on good soil in her heart. I say *chance*—but I believe, my dear Alice, that whatever utterance of mine has done good was not mine but some good word that has passed through my mind Heaven directed. Now don't fancy that I fancy I have been *inspired!* No—but to us all come thoughts we know not whence nor whither they go—nor how commissioned. She left here in January or February of 1838. She and your [great] uncle Robert were mutually interested, and when she went she left him at the most prosperous period of his life, in the very first class of New York lawyers, his profession productive of respect and honor—and profit, holding a high social position, and as it seemed to me essential to my happiness, to my life. On the ninth of the following March he was struck down by the apoplexy and consequent paralysis, and from that time his life declined. This was the first news from us that reached our friend. In May 1839 we (your [great] uncle and aunt, cousin Maria, Lizzie, your mother, and I) went to Europe. Mrs. J. received me with the warmth of a true friend. She was then living at St. John's Wood near London with her father, a paralytic but still a jovial Irishman (and all her unmarried family). He had been an accomplished painter and attached to the Court of George III. I remember well his cordial salutation and his saying (with a kind reference to my little book and to his own consolations) "Miss Sedgwick, *I* am the rich poor man" and saying so he looked with overflowing eyes upon his devoted wife, whom I always found sitting beside him, and on Mrs. Jameson, who was truly his joy and pride and support.[79] She had two unmarried sisters, and finally one widowed one and for the support of them all she labored, as Mrs. [Fanny] Kemble says, valiantly to the last. I have never seen her since our parting when we left England for the Continent, though from that time till within a year or two we have maintained our correspondence, she always writing more promptly than I, simply from my conviction that I could give her no adequate return. She sent me her beautiful books from time to time—love tokens which were taken impulsively from her room or table as she was parting from some friend coming here. The engraved name I use for my books she made for me. She drew the vignette and engraved it while she was shut up with her father during his last sickness. She worked a worsted cushion for me, sent me a volume of poetry from Miss Baillies library, and two letter presses that had long been in her own use.[80] I mention this to you, Alice, to show the steadiness of her feeling for me. I cherish this remembrance, for the impression she made was of an impulsive person whose affections would be rather showers than fountains. The engraving of her in my room was from a picture painted by her father long before I knew her. As I knew her, her expression was subdued—the hope, the proud casting of her future life were gone. There were lines of suffering, and a softness that comes as much from sympathy as suffering. She had a pale, clear, intellectual blue eye that could flash anger or jealousy or love. Her hair was red, and her complexion very fair and of the hue of an irate temper. Her arms, neck, and hands were beautiful, but her whole person wanted dignity. It was short and of those dimensions that to ears polite are embonpoint, to the vulgar fat. Her genius and accomplishments need no note of mine. They live in her books. I believe no woman has written more variously and few, men or women, so well. She impressed me as the

[79]Sedgwick had published the highly didactic tale *The Poor Rich Man, and the Rich Poor Man* in 1836.

[80]The Scottish poet and playwright Joanna Baillie (1762–1851) was a contemporary of Jameson. After publishing her first volume of poems in 1790, Baillie's series of plays began to appear eight years later. She continued to publish plays for the next four decades.

best talker I ever heard—and I have heard many gifted "unknown" and many known and celebrated. Mrs. Kemble, who has had far more extended opportunties than mine as she has been familiar with men trained to talk in the London social arena, I have heard assign the first place to Mrs. Jameson. Her gifts and accomplishments are not now mere laurels on her grave, but have passed on as I trust to a higher sphere. And above them all the crown of her filial piety.

April 24th [1860]—I go on, dear Alice, with my narrative. I was thirteen years old when I went to Albany. My brother Theodore had just opened an office there and formed his partnership with Harmanus Bleecker, a gentleman of the pure old Holland stock, a gentleman in his education, association, and tastes. He had a ruling taste for mental pursuits and was loyal to them all his life. He was silent and laconic but delighted in a social atmosphere. He was all his life compared to such old Romans as have illustrated the sterner virtues. Of him more hereafter.

The circumstance most exciting to me in this part of my life was my father coming to Albany and taking me to Canandaigua, N.Y., then a weekly journey; now scarcely eight hours! But oh, the pleasant vicissitudes of that long travel—the disastrous chances of bad taverns and the felicity of good ones, the unexpected meeting with old friends and the making new ones, and the delightful novelty of the every day of a first journey. We traveled in a charming easy carriage (probably English-built), a phaeton which my father had already possessed many years. It was so high that, as I recall it, it seems as if, like Homer's divinities, we had made a halt in mid-air. We had excellent horses, and a house-servant, Cato. (Poor fellow! he ended his life in our state's prison.) We were the first half day toiling through the sands between Albany and Schenectady. There an old gentleman, Glen,[81] my father's comrade in Congress, came to the inn and dined with us, and my father and he sat over their

[81]Federalist Henry Glen (1739–1814) served in the United States House of Representatives from 1793 to 1801, the same decade in which Sedgwick achieved prominence in Congress.

cigars and wine till the heat of the summer's day subsided, when we mounted into our phaeton and proceeded to a little Dutch inn on the Mohawk, a few miles' drive. I don't know whether I had from nature a susceptibility to natural beauty and thus slid into communion with her, or whether I had imbibed it from my family. I think it is not common for young persons at thirteen to receive positive happiness and ineffaceable impressions from nature, [but] pictures were then daguerreotyped upon my memory that have never faded. Our first evening, sitting out on the back "stoop" of our inn, overlooking a meadow sloping down to the Mohawk, a new moon, and the leaves just quivering in its light, hundreds of fireflies glancing through the air and sparkling in the grass, the firmament clear and bright with stars, and my dear father sitting by me with his cigar, in a serene obliviousness of all mortal ill, and an effusion of affection that was his "magnetism"—this may be the heavenly state before we make acquaintance with the faculties and conditions of a more expanded life.

Thursday 26 April 1860—My last day at Woodbourne. Sydney Smith well says that it is one of the pains of old age that whatever we do carries with it the melancholy thought of being "for the last time." Surely my experience of the infinite bounty and goodness of God should fill my heart with gratitude for the past and trust for the future. I came here on the twenty-third of December. I have had since uninterrupted health (save my habitual pains). I have had the love and tender care of every member of this dear family—and troops of affectionate friends, no serious illness or overcasting sorrow among them. I have had the prime enjoyment of Mrs. Kemble's readings and her society, and many social pleasures. I have been surrounded with beautiful [moments?].

Two friends have "passed on"—Eliza Follen, whose whole life has beautiful humanity, and whose steady friendship and delightful companionship has enriched many years of my life. We were both past thirty when I first knew her. She was three years older than I. Mrs. Jameson's death I have already spoken of.

Journal

Having spent the autumn of 1826 in Boston, Sedgwick made this entry shortly before her departure. An evening spent with a friend whom she had known since childhood led Catharine to consider the difference the previous two decades had made in the lives of her father, her brothers, and herself. Robert and Harry, the brothers to whom she is referring, were living in New York City. The eldest brother, Theodore, had established himself at the family's home in Stockbridge. Charles, Sedgwick's youngest sibling, had settled in neighboring Lenox. When Sedgwick made her earlier visit to the home of Caroline Tucker Andrews she was sixteen, the same age at which her autobiography concludes.

[Fall 1826]: Saturday P.M. went to see my old friend Caroline Tucker now Andrews. I paused at her Father's house which looks now precisely as it did twenty years ago—and how painful the visions it summons. Then were the kind father and mother and five daughters in the bloom and beauty of life. There was I with my beloved Father still in the strength and happiness of his earthly existence—my two Brothers in the exuberant spirits of dawning mankind and I simple, careless, and enthusiastic, my simplicity unimpaired by experience, my enthusiasm unabated—it is still I think unquenched by experience! Since that period what changes! One single feeble scion remains of all this happy hospitable family. My father's honorable and blessed life has long been closed. My gay, boyish brothers are in the sober meridian of life—transplanted to another State—Husbands and Fathers. Thank God they have more than realized the promise of their youth.

During the same autumn, Sedgwick visited Hannah Adams, the first American woman to support herself as a writer. The author of religious and secular histories, Adams was a member of Boston's intellectual elite. Sedgwick's description highlighted Adams's long-standing engagement with books, an engagement that she obviously shared with her male colleagues. Sedgwick also mentioned Adams's spinning wheel, just as obviously emblematic of more traditional female undertakings. The juxtaposition of these two artifacts suggested the competing de-

mands made upon any nineteenth-century woman who had ambitions as an intellectual.

[17 November 1826]: Made a visit to Miss Hannah Adams—through rain and wind. She is now past seventy. Was endowed with a strong mind and quick observation, and has preserved the simplicity and innocence of a child. She said, "I read Milton, and could repeat almost the whole of it at eight years. I did not understand it, but I enjoyed it." Her childhood was so sickly that her family had no idea of saving her. She spun on a little wheel, but not the great wheel, for what was the use of teaching Hannah?

In an entry describing the stroke that her sister Eliza had suffered in 1827, Sedgwick eulogized a sibling who had provided care and affection during her early childhood. She also recorded the financial reverses that had forced her brother Harry and his wife, Jane, to move from New York City to Stockbridge. Their departure saddened Sedgwick for a number of reasons, not least because she had spent her winters in the City with them. Her brother Robert and his family now welcomed her into their household. Eliza, whom Sedgwick described elsewhere as "mother—sister—friend," died four months after Sedgwick made this entry. Harry's failing eyesight signaled the deteriorating health that ended his life less than five years later. Only after she had spent most of the entry describing the misfortunes of her siblings did Sedgwick note almost parenthetically that her third novel had been published that spring.

10 June [1827]: My dear sister Eliza, the eldest of our house, has been touched by the hand of God with a severe malady. The paralysis has been slight, and has left her faculties unimpaired, and she appears now to be regaining her usual strength. To her, sickness and death might come, without a shock. She can look back upon a life in which her duties have been well sustained—a path brightened by all the offices of a child of God. She has been an example of a Christian daughter and *sister*—wife and mother—friend and benefactor.

And now if called upon to retire from the active duties of life may she not say "here am I Lord"! . . .

My dear brother Harry is plunged into deep calamity. The unfortunate issue of one or two speculations have embarrassed his small property—the utter disappointment of long cherished and extravagant hopes has cast him into deep gloom. The situation of his eyes, rather growing worse than better, deprives him of the power of present occupation, and threatens him with one of the severest calamities that flesh is heir to. Jane—ever prompt and resolute, and with an angelic buoyancy of spirit, has risen above the waves of trouble—has, within the last week, closed her family concerns for the present, and gone with her husband to [Stockbridge] that sweet retreat where peace, love, and cheerfulness have ever reigned. But who or what can give light to the darkened mind?—peace to the troubled spirit? Thou canst, oh God—and to thee I appeal. Open again the bright fountains of cheerfulness—sustain the drooping mind—lift him up who is bowed down, and enable us all to realize that "Happy are those who *endure*."

For myself I have left forever one of the happiest and dearest homes that ever was given out of a father's house. What recollections of kindness, of love, and of enjoyment crowd on my mind. My dear Jane and I have lived in the sweetest union, and I do not think that an angel in Heaven could more perfectly perform all the offices of love and tenderness than she has done. Surely, my brother and sister, you may close the doors of that home with cheerful and grateful hearts, a home that has never closed its doors against one that could there receive your bounty and kindness. I desire to look back on the past with deep and prevailing gratitude—on the present without repining or disquiet of any kind—and to the future not only without apprehension but with a just and humble confidence that He who hath hitherto helped me will provide for me to the end. This is my desire and prayer. I feel my weakness—and thank God I feel also my strength—strength in my dependence on Him whose grace is sufficient.

My dear Robert and Elizabeth have opened their doors to me and offered me a home for life. If we are to be so united, may we all be enabled to perform our relative duties. . . . I have written thus far without even thinking that among the events of the last three months is the publication of *Hope Leslie*—from which my fond friends expect a great accession of fame to me—fame—what is it? the breath of man. Oh God let me look to thee for my approbation! May it go forth with thy blessing and produce some good feeling. I have written the greater part of it since the middle of January, but the materials were all in preparation. The booksellers are to give me $1100 for this edition of 2,000.

During the summer of 1827, Sedgwick took a holiday at Saratoga Springs, New York. Hope Leslie's *immediate success brought its author much more visibility than her earlier novels,* A New England Tale *(1822) and* Redwood *(1824). Sedgwick felt ambivalent about this response. Her relentless honesty made her acknowledge the pleasure of distinction. But that pleasure was complicated by a discomfort generated by more than undue modesty. Visibility entailed what her brother Charles aptly termed "Lafayettism," a condition in which the subject became the possession of the public. Sedgwick's lingering elitism sparked her resistance to the claims that an increasingly aggressive public made upon its famous. Conventions of gender that defined fame as unfeminine deepened that resistance.*

[Summer 1827]: I was introduced to multitudes at the Springs who paid this compliment to what they deemed my literary success. It would be difficult for me, even in the quiet retirement where vanity is stripped of its illusion, to balance justly the advantages and disadvantages of the little notoriety I have attained. I have prayed earnestly, and earnestly endeavored to escape the intoxication of flattery. I am aware that it is perfectly empty—that half who administer to my vanity do it to gratify their own. I sometimes perceive an honest, heartfelt emotion and I am touched by it, as when a lovely woman said to me, "I thought when I saw you I must embrace you." I do not disguise from myself that I feel a pleasure in being able to command a high station wherever I go, and that I often enjoy the power of being able to gratify others by notice and attention. But I feel deeply the disadvantage of what my sweet, modest Charles calls "Lafayettism" on a very humble scale, being the quest and profession of the public and being obliged to fritter away in general, transient courtesies time and thought and feeling. I am conscious that what distinction I have attained is greatly owing to the paucity of our literature, and I have another powerful preservative against undue self-complacency in the consciousness that whatever talent I have shown is the original gift of God, that it is not my own—and has not been improved by industry and careful cultivation as it should—that I have more cause to mourn over what I have not done than to exult in what I have done—more cause for humility than for pride.

The praise for Hope Leslie *continued unabated, as did Sedgwick's ambivalence about her recognition. Inveterately modest in evaluating her contributions to a fledgling American literature, she claimed relatively little for herself. Readers and critics disagreed, insisting that Sedgwick be ranked with contemporaries James Fenimore Cooper, Washington Irving, and William Cullen Bryant. Sedgwick measured her novels, tales, and sketches against a prevailing standard that made aesthetic and moral criteria equally important. Other members of her literary generation did the same. Sedgwick was nonetheless exceptional in the importance she attached to this dual purpose.*

27 [August 1827]: I have received a host of letters the past week filled with affection, kindness, and compliment—one from Mr. [William Ellery] C[hanning] which has gratified me exceedingly—his approbation is worth all the trouble *all* my literary labor has cost me. Then how far are my present rewards beyond my desserts. Have I not reason to fear that I have my *good things here?* My continual prayer to God is that I may be enabled by the aids of his gracious spirit to resist pride, vanity, egotism, self-complacency, and all those selfish propensities and emotions to which I am too much inclined

and to which my success and the partiality of my friends so much expose me. May I measure what I have done by what I ought to have done. May I remember that the talent, one or ten, is the gift of God, the improvement only mine. May I compare myself with those who are unknown to the world—unpraised—unsought—and in whom I see a quiet virtue—a humility—Christian submission and love that rebukes me. I made a visit yesterday to a poor, solitary, infirm old woman—weak and ignorant to the last degree—and yet I saw in her a confidence in the good providence of God that cometh not by wisdom—a *principled and cheerful* submission to evils, which I felt that I could not thus endure. My life is too much one of indulgence and excitement. May the grace of God counteract this.

Lauded as the signal text for those in pursuit of power, Niccolo Machiavelli's The Prince *failed to impress Sedgwick. The reason was simple—Machiavelli, the Italian political theorist of the early sixteenth century, insisted that virtue and power were incompatible, an idea that Sedgwick considered pernicious. In rejecting his premises, Sedgwick aligned herself with an eighteenth-century model that validated the exercise of power for the benefit of society rather than self. It was telling that Sedgwick damned Machiavelli at the very moment in which an increasingly popular individualism privileged a model that sanctioned the pursuit of self-interest. Sedgwick's convictions were informed by the past and the present. Her insistence upon the disinterested exercise of power reflected the still salient influence of her father. But her posture was just as deeply marked by the gender conventions of her own century. Constructed as masculine, the pursuit of self-interest was juxtaposed against a selflessness that was celebrated as feminine. Both of these influences shaped the perspective Sedgwick brought to her literary career.*

6 September [1827]: I have just finished Machiavelli's *Prince*. The Edinburgh Review is (I think) right about him as about most things. Machiavelli seems to me to have considered virtue and

power incompatible and merely to have intended to teach the children of this world how to be wise in their generation. He makes his Prince a perfectly selfish being—in the bad sense of selfishness. His only calculation must be to preserve his power, and for this purpose he proposes such rules as this: "whoever is the occasion of another's advancement, is the cause of his own diminution." Why does he commend Caesar Borgia?[1] Not for being good, but securing success—and after all the example seems to me to refute Machiavelli's whole system—for what end could be more miserable than Borgia's?

Only four months after Sedgwick had described her sister's stroke, Eliza was dead. Her death made Sedgwick reflect upon her sister's life and the ties that bound all the siblings together.

21 October [1827]: My sister—my beloved sister Eliza is gone—that faithful, tender, religious spirit has passed to rest. The bond that has bound us together is broken, and one of our number is gone. A fountain of love and happiness is forever closed. To me she has been mother—sister—friend. She is removed from my sight, but I have a strong feeling of her existence and her presence and more vivid, more precious, than ever is the belief that we have a life that death cannot touch—over which the grave has no power. . . . I have known no life that has been from its beginnning to its close such a *domestic blessing.* Her discretion, thoughtfulness, and fidelity made her the trust of her parents in her early years—the support of my dear mother through many years of infirmity and sickness. Her discretion, sedateness, gentleness, and diligence were rare virtues in a young girl and qualified her to be an efficient support to her mother. She married at the age of twenty-two and removed to Al-

---

[1]Machiavelli's praise notwithstanding, most commentators portrayed his contemporary, the consummately ambitious Caesar Borgia (1475 or 1476–1507), as decidedly unscrupulous. They also agreed with Sedgwick about his fate. Initially, Borgia's attempt to carve a principality for himself from territories controlled by the Roman Catholic Church was successful. But Borgia's opponents forced his retreat. Sent to Spain, he was imprisoned there for two years and then was killed in a battle.

bany [and] from this time her cares accumulated. Naturally of a timid and apprehensive character and of a delicate constitution, she has suffered much, which the constant kindness of her husband could not avert. For many years her spirit was bowed down by the gloomy doctrines of Calvinism—and she has often said to me that words could not express her happiness in her deliverance from them.

Sedgwick's decision to remain single was unusual during a century in which nine out of ten women married. She cared little about whether or not she was a statistical oddity. But throughout her life Sedgwick did ponder the implications of her choice. Her reflections provide an opportunity to consider the experience of nineteenth-century women, unmarried and married.

18 May [1828]: I will not say with the ungracious poet that I turn from what spring brings to what she cannot bring, but alas, I find there is no longer that capacity for swelling, springing, brightening joy that I once felt. Memory has settled her shadowy curtain over so much of the space of thought and hope that once to my imagination tempted me with her arch and laughing and promising face to snatch away the veil, with which she but half hid the future. Hope now seems to turn from me, and if I now and then catch some glimpses of her averted face she looks so serious, so admonitory, that I almost believe that her sister Experience, with an eye of apprehension and lips that never smile, has taken her place.

All is not right with me I know. I still build on sandy foundations. I still hope for perfection where perfection is not given. The best sources of Earthly happiness are not within my grasp. Those of contentment I have neglected. I have suffered for the whole winter a sort of mental paralysis, and at times I have feared the disease extended to my affections. It is difficult for one who began life as I did—the primary object of affection to many—to come by degrees to be first to none—and still to have my love remain in its entire strength and craving such returns as have no substitute. How absurd, how groundless your complaint! would half a dozen voices exclaim if I ever ventured to *make* this complaint. I do not. Each one has his own point of sight. Others are not conscious (at least I believe they are not) of any diminution in their affections for me— but others have taken my place naturally and of right I allow it. It is the necessity of a solitary condition—an unnatural state. He who gave us our nature has set the solitary in families and has by an array of motives secured this sweet social compact to his children. From my own experience I would not advise any one to remain unmarried—for my experience has been a singularly happy one. My feelings have never been embittered by those slights or taunts that the repulsive and neglected have to endure. There has been no period of my life to the present moment when I might not have allied myself respectably, and to those sincerely attached to me, if I would. I have always felt myself to be an object of attention, respect, and regard—though not first to any. I am like Themistocles[2] *second* to a great many. My fortune is not adequate to an independent establishment, but it is ample for ease to myself and liberality to others. In the families of all my brothers I have an agreeable home. My sisters are all kind and affectionate to me. My brothers generous and invariably kind—their children all love me. My dear Kate, my adopted child is, though far from perfect even in my doating eyes, yet such as to perfectly satisfy me if I did not crave perfection for one I so tenderly love. I have troops of friends—some devotedly attached to me—yet the result of all this very happy experience is that there is no equivalent for those blessings which Providence has placed first and ordained that they should be purchased at the dearest sacrifice. I have not set this down in the spirit of repining— but it is well, I think honestly, to expose our own feelings. They may serve for examples or beacons. While I live I do not mean this shall be read and after, my individual experience may perhaps benefit some one of all my tribe.

---

[2]The Athenian Themistocles (c. 528–462 B.C.) sought positions of leadership throughout a long career as a statesman, but his aspirations were continually thwarted.

In an entry made while she was staying in Stockbridge, Sedgwick la-
mented her brother Harry's illness. Because she and Harry had shared
much intellectually, the shattering of his brilliant mind was almost
more than his sister could bear. Their mother, Pamela, had suffered
intermittently from a similar disorder for two decades before her death
in 1807. Sedgwick thought the parallel was coincidental, however.
Whatever the cause, there was one similarity—physicians could do
little to relieve either Pamela's or Harry's condition.

31 December 1828: To see a mind once so powerful, so effective, so
luminous—darkened—disordered—a broken instrument—to see
him stared at by the vulgar the laugh of children—oh, it is too
much. And yet his reason and his affections are struggling with this
evil. His love seems an inextinguishable light. It shines through the
darkness. Most persons no doubt consider this an hereditary malady. I think it is not so, and yet I fear to express this lest it should
be deemed a feeling of family pride. He is less like my dear mother
than any child she left physically, mentally, and morally. The energy
of his mind that if not fed with food from without consumes the
mind itself—his ardor uncontrolled—his passions for great objects—the magnificent, if I may so call it in his disposition, always
fixing on splendid projects—always anticipating brilliant results—
have been the innate causes—these set in action by external
causes—the failure of flattering speculations, the loss of sight, and
the consequent suspension from occupation. It has been enough to
work this wild desolation.

Elizabeth Freeman, whom Sedgwick and her family always called
Mumbet, played a signal role in the abolition of slavery in post-
revolutionary Massachusetts. With Theodore Sedgwick as her counsel,
Freeman challenged the constitutionality of slavery in the courts of
Berkshire County in 1781. Daughter Catharine chronicled the trial in
"Slavery in New England," a sketch which she published seventy years
later. Immediately after she achieved her freedom, Mumbet joined
Sedgwick's household in Stockbridge. Servant, companion, friend,

Mumbet stood at the center of Catharine's childhood. Her name signi-
fied a still more meaningful role—"Ma Bet" served as Catharine's
mother during the long periods in which Pamela Sedgwick was inca-
pacitated. Elizabeth Freeman's strength, decisiveness, and integrity
were the legacies that the adult Sedgwick celebrated in this entry. Free-
man died on 28 December 1829, almost exactly a month after Sedgwick
made this entry.

29 November 1829: Mumbet—"Mother"—my nurse—my faithful
friend—she who first received me into her arms—is finishing her
career—a life marked by as perfect a performance of duty—perhaps I should say more perfect than I have ever known. Her talents
were not small nor limited: a clear mind—strong judgment—a
quick and firm decision—an iron resolution—an incorruptible integrity—an integrity that never for a moment parleyed with temptation—a truth that never varied from the straight line—an unex-
ceptionable fidelity to her engagements—always as she said "up to
the mark"—a strong love of justice stern as Brutus—she could not
forgive a wrong, but she would sooner have died at the stake than
committed it—a productive, intelligent industry—an astonishing
capacity of labor and endurance—a severe economy—and
affections stronger than death were the riches of her character. She
was born in slavery and brought up by a hard, oppressive mistress.
Her master was a man of gentle mould, but as it was not the custom
of the time to have any moral intercourse with the slave or to impart
any direct instruction, her character may be said to have been impressed by Divine influence, to have been God's gift—his image.

Her spirit spurned slavery. "I would have been willing," she has
often said to me in speaking of the period when she was in hopeless
servitude, "I would have been willing if I could have had one minute of freedom—just to say '*I am free*' I would have been willing to
die at the end of that minute." With this feeling ever alive she heard
the Declaration of Independence read. "If all are free and equal,"
she said, "why are we slaves?" and at her instance my father com-
menced a suit in the Supreme Court the result of which was (I do

not understand the technical proceedings) that the blacks of the Commonwealth were restored to their natural rights—declared free. She then (forty-nine years last summer) came to my father's to live, and from that time till 1808 (the time of my father's last marriage) she lived with us with the exception of short intervals. When my father married again she felt that she could no longer maintain the authority into which she had gradually grown—and saying she "could not learn new ways" she went to live at the little place which she had earned with the sweat of her brow.

Since that time she has been occasionally with us—in our joys and our sorrows she has always been summoned as a necessary link in the family chain. She has wept and rejoiced with [us]. She has clung to us with a devotion and tenacity of love seldom equalled and we have honored her.

In 1830, Sedgwick published her fourth novel. Clarence: A Tale Of Our Own Times *represented a departure for the author. Locating her characters in a contemporary social and cultural milieu, Sedgwick presented her readers with an indictment of an increasingly materialistic America. Despite the social and cultural criticism with which* Clarence *was laced, Sedgwick was unusually confident about the novel's prospects. That confidence derived from at least two sources—a still tentative willingness to acknowledge her literary abilities and a conviction that her readers might well share her concerns about their society.*

14 May 1830: I have this morning sent the last proof sheet of "Clarence" to press. It has been an employment and sometimes a solace to me through months of various experience. . . . I am grateful to God for the health that has enabled me to support the labor of the work. I am grateful to Him for the faculties that are equal to such an employment. Any self-complacency I might feel is checked by the consciousness that my mind is God's gift and that far from improving it as I might have done, I have many a neglected talent, many a waste place. I honestly confess that I earnestly desire and hope for success and expect it—but if I am disappointed I pray to

God that I may be humble not irritated against the world—that I may have the testimony within my own soul that I have not embarked my tranquillity on the uncertain wave of popular favor but have safely anchored it in the humble hope of the approbation and acceptance of my Father in Heaven.

The status of "second best" in the affections of those to whom she was most deeply committed was inevitable for a woman who had decided to remain unmarried in the nineteenth century. Sedgwick understood that cost. What she had not anticipated was a resulting vulnerability to depression. Her literary career provided an important stimulus. Sedgwick's determined resistance was equally critical in sustaining her.

5 August [1830]: This season has *not* been a happy one to me. I have resisted a depression of spirits resulting partly from self-dissatisfaction—partly from causes independent of myself, unknown and that will be untold, but enough to give a dark hue to life—and partly from my position in life. Never perhaps was a condition of inferiority or dependence made by the affection of friends more tolerable than mine. Still I hanker after the independence and interests and power of communication of a home of my own. My feelings are often wounded—most unintentionally—and I cannot tell and ought not to feel these little rubs—but when were the feelings perfectly subordinate to duty! There is a yearning in my heart for a more intense feeling than I can ever call forth. . . . Oh this *second best* to all is a hard condition—the want of it is that depression with me, [it] brings on a sort of paralysis of mind and heart. I must have something exciting to keep alive my powers. I always become sleepy with a poor hand at cards. I do not yield to this repining without resistance or without compunction. I know what reason—what religion demands of me—and I pray to God to give a spirit of humility, of submission, of resignation.

Early in January 1831, Sedgwick journeyed to Washington. After returning at the end of the month, she recorded her impressions of the nation's Capitol—"The largest edifice I had ever seen—of white marble—on a beautiful eminence and the colors of our country—the spangled banner floating over the columns of the portico." The city's residents had welcomed the prominent author. And yet Sedgwick remained detached from the praise of those who read her fiction. The sources for her response were complicated. In part, it reflected the elitism she had inherited from her father. More significant, the reaction suggested a determined resistance to self-aggrandizement. However laudable that stance, Sedgwick's admiring public was closer to the mark in evaluating her books. The novels, tales, and sketches went far beyond the "respectable mediocrity" that Sedgwick ascribed to them.

20 February 1831: [I attended a large gathering] where a great many fashionable people were assembled—where I was introduced to many persons—but there is a balance to all the pleasure one's vanity may receive from notoriety and general introduction. You can merely exchange half a dozen conventional phrases such as "when did you come?" "are you pleased?" "how long do you stay?" and from the more common and less practiced sort of people you get an "I'm already acquainted with you thro' your books ma'am"— and it may chance a few washy compliments.

Now and then there is something that touches the finer springs. A visit from Judge [John] Marshall which I certainly in part owed to his friendship to my dear father was among the highest (no not *among*) gratifications of my visit to Washington. I do not depreciate the civilities I have received nor the ground on which they were accorded. I find my reputation far greater than I think I deserve— the world is good natured and kind hearted especially to what they consider *respectable mediocrity,* for it neither alarms their pride nor provokes their envy.

Sedgwick's visit to Washington included a call upon President Andrew Jackson. The visit led Sedgwick to reflect upon the supposed equality upon which white Americans prided themselves. Her lingering elitism was also apparent here. However, that was less important than the

critical question that Sedgwick's commentary posed—was the equality
that antebellum Americans celebrated merely rhetorical?

20 February 1831: Escorted by Mr. Secretary [Martin] Van Buren [I]
went to pay respects to the President. He received us politely—is
simple, gentlemanly, and unaffected in his manners. He looks like
a weather beaten old soldier—as if he might be thoroughly man-
aged by the "wily secretary." We were shown through the damp cold
rooms into *the* drawing room. The nation's drawing room—where
the mobocracy assemble by the light of beautiful chandeliers and
circulating amidst rich furniture—great men and accomplished
women fancy they live in a country of equality as well as liberty.
Query: do they ever feel their inequality more than on such occasions?

Sedgwick's brother Harry died on 22 December 1831, six days before her
forty-second birthday. The entry made on that birthday mourned the
brother who had been "the companion of my childhood, my youth, my
mature age." It also recorded Sedgwick's continued determination to
measure herself by a strenuous ideal.

28 December 1831: We all blessed God—for our brother. I can write
no more now. He had been dead to us for six weeks—no word, no
look of recognition—but still the face through which the spirit had
ministered remained the same. We could watch him—minister to
him—kiss him—and his countenance was so sweet—so beautiful—his sleep so gentle and now he is *gone*. In the *grave*. Oh, not
to the grave—not to the grave. The spirit is not yet there. I know it
is not—I believe—help Lord my unbelief! Monday afternoon, he
was *buried*. Dr. Flint had previously examined his head. I know not
yet the particulars of the result. I only know he was *incurable*. My
poor brother—how much have you suffered!

It is my birthday. I have not strength for the thoughts that are
suited to this period. My heart has been sent—and a portion of my
life is gone. I pray God to forgive my sins—and if more of life is
spared to me to enable me to do better in future than I have done

in the past. At another time I may record precious recollections of my brother—I have not now strength or tranquillity. My temples are beating and I have no heart, no thought.

Almost immediately after Harry's death, Sedgwick joined her brother Robert and his family in New York City. Sedgwick's niece and namesake Kate accompanied her. With this visit Kate replicated the years of her aunt's childhood that were spent in the City. Sedgwick waited until the summer to record her impressions of the previous winter.

1 July 1832: My campaign is nearly ended—another six months gone and I trust though very incompetently filled it has not been wasted. My dear Kate—with what grateful joy do I make this entry—has diligently employed her winter—has improved all her opportunties—has received the approbation of all her teachers—and has won the love of her Uncle [Robert] and Aunt [Elizabeth] and their approbation. For myself I would devoutly thank God for this rich and sweet gift. . . . My time has been filled by small but I trust not profitless occupation. I think I have been of some use to my dear Jane [Harry's widow], and it is now an essential part of my plan of life to benefit those dear children who have through both parents such claims on me. The illusions of life are I think pretty much gone. Some of its treasures are gone.

The death of the novelist Sir Walter Scott prompted a eulogistic entry in Sedgwick's journal. Sedgwick's respect was apparent, as was the unparalleled popularity of Scott among nineteenth-century Americans.

17 November 1832: Sir Walter Scott, our friend our benefactor, is no more. He has gone down to the grave with all that the world could render of honor and love. His spirit still survives and pervades the civilized world. He is the companion of the aged and the young—the light of our social life—the solace of our solitude—the staff of the aged—the comforter of the sick—the instructor of the young—mastering every spring, and half forming the instrument on which he plays at will.

Exactly one year after Harry's death, Sedgwick recalled how much he had meant to her. All of Sedgwick's brothers had provided support for their sister's career. But it was Harry who had printed her poetry when she was still an adolescent, Harry who had encouraged her to turn to fiction, Harry who had interceded with editors and publishers. His death, then, had consequences that extended beyond the sorrow that Sedgwick inscribed in this entry. The continued publication of novels, tales, and sketches testified to his early influence, to Sedgwick remaining "faithful to your memory." But, as she acknowledged, with his death "one of the great spurs to effort" had also died. In another entry written two months later, Sedgwick made clear how difficult she found the challenge. Nonetheless, she persisted, although the trajectory of her career changed. Having published four novels in the nine years before Harry's death, she wrote only two more in the next twenty-five years. Her publication of tales and sketches continued unabated, however.

23 December 1832: This is the anniversary of my dear brother's death. How vividly has memory presented to me that day of anguish. I have lived it over again—but softened by time, by a more grateful sense of the mercy that closed his life without more physical suffering—and I think with a more distinct anticipation of a reunion. I seem sometimes to catch the glimmering light of another morning. My dear Harry, my heart has been faithful to your memory. I think of you. I sorrow and rejoice over my past relations with you many and many hours when none can fathom the secret musing of my spirit. Life is changed to me. One of the great spurs to effort is gone. I am loved and cherished but I believe there is none now that loves me with that partial and proud affection that you once loved me with. They have all *dearer* objects. They have not the same sympathy with me. I do not blame them. God forbid I have more than I deserve—but no words can tell—no thought can reach to the feeling I have of loss counting what you, my dear Harry, were to me before your dreadful afflictions came upon you.

13 February [1833]: I am doubting whether at once resolutely to

sacrifice my Ms. or to go on and see if I can get a moment of inspiration, a starting point. If I had spirit to enter on a new career I would. History, biography anything seems now to me more attractive than this "heavy work."

Like so many others who met her, Sedgwick was fascinated by the English actress Fanny Kemble. Kemble's reputation as a remarkable performer had been established before 1832, the year the twenty-two-year-old actress began a highly successful tour in the United States. Her marriage to slaveholding planter Pierce Butler ended her career, at least temporarily. But she returned to the stage in both the United States and England after she and her husband separated in 1845. Following her divorce four years later, Kemble made Lenox, Massachusetts, one of her residences. Sedgwick's enduring friendship with Kemble dates from the meeting described in this entry.

14 February [1833]: I passed last evening with Fanny Kemble at Mrs. Bells. Nature made her a gem and art has given her its highest polish but nature, beautiful nature, peers over art—or rather is the creator and art but the humble instrument. She appears to me to love what is simple—to aim to be true—or to be so impulsively. She lives in a cloud of incense and yet seems not to be blinded and to be so accustomed to it that she sees truly through a false medium. This shows a well adjusted lens in the mental eye. She dances with the glee of unbroken youth. She sings with dramatic effect. Never have I before seen a person that justified (and she does fully) that beautiful description "each look each motion waked a newborn grace/That o'er her form its transient glory cast/Some lovelier wonder soon usurp'd its place/Chas'd by a charm still lovelier than the last." Am I wrong in giving so much time and thought to her? My conscience is *not easy*—and yet I think that she who kindles the evening with the brightness that lit up the morning of life, who brings a melting influence to the frigid of forty, is an enchantress not to be resisted.

[13 April 1833]: I remember little of the few days past but those bright points that Fanny K. like a sun has illuminated and made so dazzling as to cast all others into shadow. I parted with her today. There is infinite zest in her society. I may be disappointed in her, but if it is illusion I hope it will last. My vanity is not bribed, for she says nothing to propitiate it. I perceive that her feelings—her attachments—her prejudices are all English—but I believe she is true. I know she is nature's cunning workmanship—a creature richly gifted by her Creator—and as yet the gifts are not melted down and run in the worn mould of custom.

In this entry, Sedgwick imagined herself as responding to a foreigner's inquiries about antebellum America's largest city. Sedgwick's keen sense of the conventions by which members of New York City's elite governed themselves is everywhere apparent, as is her ability to elaborate upon their implications. The richly textured description highlights those conventions that served as primary signifiers of status. Ironically, the prevailing ideology of egalitarianism made these markers of status all the more necessary. Sedgwick's description suggests as well the singular power of gender in shaping the behavior of antebellum Americans.

[11 May 1833]: Let me see how I would describe the society of New York if I were writing to a correspondent abroad. My dear M—, You would have some account of the society—so called of this great city. This is not easy to give with truth. The population is so multifarious and changing that compared with other cities it is somewhat like the ocean—constant in nothing but change compared with the comparatively inflexible features of the solid earth.

The most stable circle is the "privileged," lauded and caricatured as "good society" till the term has become of doubtful import. The good society is of course the fashionable, and with a very few exceptions—as must always be the case in a commercial metropolis, the rich. This class is of course aristocratical and exclusive as far as in their ties. If they were not so they must be exceptions to the general law that makes every human being seek after something that his neighbor has not. This is the spring of all effort, whether the impulse directs to being a Statesman or a Philanthropist or leading the fashions of a great city. Giving brilliant parties and visiting all the visitable is that which the individual character must decide. I am afraid our "good society" resembles a little too much the parvenus of your country, people who feel themselves standing on such uncertain, slippery ground that they fear to stretch out a hand to help another *up* lest they should go *down*. Your real aristocracy, I take it, live in a fortress, quite fearless, and leave to the *mercenaries* the care of defending the outposts. Those who maintain their places most gracefully on their eminence are those who feel most secure there. For the most part [they are] those who have been there longest. Our most fashionable society consists chiefly of natives of the city and Foreigners. I think there is some little jealousy of interlopers from other states, particularly from New England. Foreigners obtain an entrée with great facility and are not unfrequently obliged to make a forced exit.

The gay season begins about the middle of December and lasts till the middle of March. Dinner parties, including ladies, excepting a few given to strangers are rare. Déjeunés [luncheons] almost unknown. The commonest mode of society is a large evening party. I think an ambition for numbers is not yet excessive. The guests on an invitation of from a week to ten days assemble about ten o'clock, an hour by the way quite unnecessarily late and imitative of European manners—our [citizen's?] family dinner being from three to four there is no need of advancing the evening party into the night. On entering the house the ladies are shown upstairs into a cloak room, the gentlemen to another. Here they adjust themselves for presentment in the drawing room and meet again at the staircase. In case it is a regular ball the carpets are removed from the drawing rooms. The dancing commences immediately—cotillions, waltzes, the Spanish dance, the gallopade, and the mazurka are danced. Wine, cake, and lemonade are served during the evening. About twelve a general murmur announces the supper and the company throng to the supper room. There a long table is spread. The gentlemen serve the ladies and then themselves, the servants only interposing to take away discarded plates, glasses, etc. The fare is more or less elegant according to the taste of the entertainer and sometimes various and abounding in "les choses superflus si necessaires!" [the things so superfluous, so necessary], according to their wealth. But this accordance is not severe. "Everybody" has oysters, ham, tongue, ice, blancmange, jelly, sweetmeats, Mother's cake, fruit, and champagne. These are the necessaries. Then à discrétion are the boned turkies, the delicate birds, truffles, the pyramids of confitures in their veils of crystallized sugar, the baskets of delicate confectionary filled with sugar fruit, the Chateau Margaud, Burgundy, and German wines. Man is an eating animal, and where society has not arrived to that degree of refinement in which all natural propensities are hidden, a luxurious supper will be a circumstance in his daily existence. I have not any country but my own, but I confess that the empressement with which the young men sometimes jostle one another at the supper table has annoyed me—and it is frequently the subject of remark.

It is obvious that this mode of entertainment has many disadvantages. It cuts hospitality up by the roots—indeed it is a common and not more than a demi-satirical remark in what our English visitors consider our demi-civilized society that hospitality is the virtue of barbarians. Another equally manifest and perhaps more serious disadvantage is that the ball or crowded party is only adapted to the young, gay, and dancing part of the population. The fathers and mothers are mere spectators, driven to the wall, and feeling themselves to be mere furniture and sometimes lumber they desire on any pretext to stay at home. A married woman past thirty in America is the same nonentity that a French girl of sixteen is— but the one is sustained by hope. She is looking into a world in which she is to be an actor. Our poor married lady has played out the play, and what [is] so dull as a theater when the curtain has fallen! The sons and daughters are abandoned on the threshold of society, and our drawing rooms want the softening effect of blended colors. They are all glare and noise. Our men of business—it must be remembered that all our men (with the exception of some half a dozen idlers who not being enough to form a class are like drift-wood at the mercy of every chance current) are workers. The law-yer, the physician, the clergyman, the merchant, the man of letters after a hard day's work are in no humor to dress themselves to ap-pear in a drawing room at ten where there is nothing for them—no new form of excitment to restore the tone of their overtasked spirits and where in their vacuity they feel that "it *is* misery to do or *suffer* wealthy."

An effort was made some three or four years ago by half a dozen families of haut ton [high tone] to introduce a more rational form of entertainment. They assembled at eight—had a single violin for the dancers, and lemonade, sugar, and water for refreshment. This was a leap from the Equator to the Pole. Our young gallants are no anchorites, they denounced their potation, and caricatured them. I remember seeing a pretty good caricature of a beau falling into the arms of two others, too weak to sustain him, all evidently dying of inanition. The reformed soirées ended with the gay season and were never resumed.

Recently there has been a more rational and far more promising attempt at a social improvement. A lady who has been some years abroad, and who has seen more of the privileged classes than often falls to the lot of Americans, has returned, and being mistress of a fine mansion and ample fortune and benevolently inclined to dis-pense to others the forms of happiness she has herself enjoyed, opens her house every Wednesday evening. Her acquaintance ex-tends through the whole circle of fashion in the City. But she does not limit the entrée to her soirées to these passe partouts [pass keys]. She has an honorable ambition of assembling about her whatever there is of talent or accomplishment in the City, whether bearing the brand of good society or not. She has hinted and said that she would prefer her guests should come in the half dress cus-tomary in the French soirées, but this to our ladies who make the toilet science their chief study (of course after their school days) was the lemonade regimen, and they still appear in their ball dresses. There is *no* dancing. Music occasionally and from the very best amateurs. No refreshments handed about, but a refreshment room above to which the visitors repair whenever the body, not the spirit, moves. There is a table, too, where tea and coffee are served by pretty, neat women, and where there is an abundant supply of ices, cakes, and sweetmeats. Wine and lemonade [are] on a side table. This is certainly a great refinement on common modes of entertainment, and as the lady's standing, fortune, and [an] acknowledged munificence give her authority, we trust her retrenchment will be imitated—and still more that she will be emulated in her ambition of making a circulating medium from the rich mines among us.

Shortly after she had recorded her observations about New York City's elite, Sedgwick traveled to Virginia. Her visit there provided a comparative dimension by which she measured New England's villages. No regional chauvinist, Sedgwick was ready to judge the rural South on its own merits. But seeing those who were enslaved made that judgment damning. Sedgwick's second entry concerned the impact of slavery on those who supposedly benefitted from the peculiar institution.

27 June 1833: [Having arrived at the "plantation tavern" where they were to spend the night, Sedgwick describes a setting in which] the birds are singing. The clouds have melted away. The air is serene. It is a sweet, quiet spot. The harvest is in stacks, the turf clean, and the little negroes of all shades trotting over it looking decently clad. I miss the busy villages of New England, but if it were not for this horrid stain—this misery of slavery—I think I should prefer this solitary rural life. No I should not. The negro huts look comfortable, and if they were free and the masters not masters but protectors this might be made to realize the beau ideal of proprietor and cultivator.

8 July 1833: The Virginians seem content with the Patrician or Aristocratic power that results to them from their being slave-holders.

The white is the Patrician color, and there is a much more perfect equality among the whites than with us. Our landlord and his family sit at the table with us. The drivers too. A driver replied to Doctor B. (who was finding fault with him) as if he were no subject of reprehension, "Sir, I am a white man." That principle of self-interest and self-pushing, which has some odious aspects, results in such great good to our communities at the North—is such a steam power to the great machine of society—that we may submit to the petty evils that result from it. A Virginian, accustomed from the effect of slavery to sitting with one, sometimes both hands hid, all his life suffers from year to year evils that a Yankee would not endure for a day—broken door-steps—broken windows—no blinds—rutty, *rocky* post roads intersected with the roots and dotted with the stumps of old trees in this age of canals and railroads. This mode of living sparsely on plantations keeps back the improvements of society, the betterment of social life. The lord of the soil lives in coarse plenty—and with the wide power of a highland chieftain—surrounded by his dependents and slaves, but he has none of the arts and luxuries that result from independent, individual talent, interests, and necessities combined for the general good. Compare the best Virginia plantation to the smallest village in New England—with its shops, its artisans, its minister, and schoolhouse.

In one of the longest entries in her journal, Sedgwick, a Unitarian, described an evangelical who was holding a revival in Stockbridge. Sedgwick's hostility to the Calvinism he preached was to be expected. More than a decade before, she had abandoned what she described as the "'you can and you can't' system" of orthodox Congregationalism. But the sharp edge of her remarks derived more from the itinerant minister's "new measures" than the message itself. Sedgwick's focus upon the women involved in the revival reflected an antebellum social reality—women outnumbered men in the nation's churches and reviv-

als. She attended the revival with two other skeptics, her friend Sarah
Ashburner and her niece Maria Banyer Sedgwick.

29 September 1833: It is now about three weeks since a man by the
name of Foote came into our immediate neighborhood to hold
what is called a protracted meeting. He is what is called a *new-
measure* man—dissenting from the orthodox Calvinists in some
points. The only material one as far as I know is that the sinner has
the power of resolving to be a Christian and that this resolution
makes him one. This is certainly an improvement upon the "you
can and you can't" system. But it is only in the theory of the religion. In the application Foote seems as fanatical and far more
coarse and revolting than any other usurper of the holy office we
have ever had among us. His mode of proceeding is to terrify the
subject, appall the imagination with hell fire, and then present his
patent machine of a *resolve*. He is a singularly wolfish looking person—with black eyes, brows, and hair to match—a vulgar nose—
a mouth of the demoniacal order—thin lips—closing firmly and
when opening disclosing black and broken teeth the decay of humanity somewhat deducting from the pure fiend. He is lank and
attenuated in his person. I should think not a hypocrite, for he is as
bold and dauntless as Milton's Satan. He is full of tricks—insolent
stares—violent changes of the voice—from a whisper to a
scream—furious gesticulation, etc. His subjects are of all ages from
children of four years—for at that age I heard him say they should
be pressed into the Kingdom of Heaven. I heard him once at [the
neighboring community of] Lee. One story he told struck me as
betraying the engines with which he worked. He said "there is a
young woman in this place—not far from here—who is in great
distress of mind. A young man—a friend (I don't remember his
words but they implied he was her lover) made her pledge herself
by a promise that she would not go near protracted meetings. Her
friend has gone from here. She is anxious, but she fears to come
because she is bound by her pledge. I fear she has sold her soul to

the devil, and that her friend will return and find her in her coffin and death written on her forehead!!" Of course, this was reported to the girl—her conscience already alarmed—and if she chances to have a lively imagination the coffin and the sentence of eternal death may realize the prophecy or drive her to insanity.

On Saturday Sarah A[shburner], Maria [Banyer Sedgwick],[3] and myself went to Wetmore's where, as we had heard, an anxious meeting[4] was to be holden. The people were collected in great numbers when we arrived—wagons driving up at any moment filled with young persons—principally females. There were very few there past thirty. The rooms and entry were already pretty well filled. We were met at the door by a pert looking little fellow who seemed to dilate with the consciousness of his brief authority. "Are you a professor?" he asked Sarah. . . . "Not of this religion," she replied. "Of what then?" "I am a Christian." "Have you been born again?" "Stuff!" said Sarah turning away from him, whereupon seeing that the magnificent creature before him was no material for his moulding he pertly told her that [this] was no place for her for he saw "the impress of the devil on her heart." He then began to question me—and Foote himself, probably perceiving it was a case for the master's handling, came forward and addressed to me the usual interrogations. I replied that we were not "anxious sinners" but persons curious to witness the proceedings of an "anxious meeting." Whereupon he became savage—told us in the harshest, violent manner to go away for that was no place for "laughing, curious sinners!" Mr. Churchill met me. I spoke to him as usual and he in his same friendly manner gave me his hand. "Don't speak to that woman," screamed Foote and Churchill dropped my hand as if he had been shot. Some others spoke to me. "Hold no conversation with that

---

[3]A fellow resident of Stockbridge and long-standing friend of the Sedgwicks, Sarah Ashburner shared Catharine Maria Segwick's religious sentiments. Maria Banyer Sedgwick, also a resident of Stockbridge, was the daughter of Theodore and Susan Ridley Sedgwick.

[4]Designed to generate an intense desire for salvation, the anxious meeting focused upon the peril of sin, the requirement of repentance, and the saving character of conversion.

woman!" reiterated the master and the obedient slaves dispersed. "Don't pray for that woman," cried Foote, pouring out his last vial. Some questions were speared at Maria, who had a much more serious, saintly look than Sarah or I—but she replied with a quiet dignity that she wished to have no discussions.

We retired without the yard and remained standing by the fence observing as far as we could through the open windows the proceedings and making serious comments to such persons as now and then joined us. One was little, smiling Eliza Ferry, who was pressing into the worship but gave her usual good natured greeting, another a poor little poppinjay who came. Turned out of the house because he would not kneel and confess his sins, he came half-scared and half-indignant but finding us to listen and sympathize he soon talked himself into a triumphant confessor. A party of two ladies and one man alighted in their passage to the house stopped to listen to our remarks. I was contrasting Foote's proceeding with the gentleness of him who came to seek and to save those who were lost. One of the women advanced and told me I had wrong impressions of Mr. Foote, that she was his companion and knew him well. I did not think of the technical meaning of *companion*—and I proceeded to say what must have seemed hard to conjugal ears (however verified by conjugal experience) carefully confining my strictures to what I had seen and heard. Sarah handled the subject without mittens, but a man telling [her] who Mrs. Foote was she begged her pardon. These women proceeded to the usual coarse remarks upon our unchristian state and Mrs. Foote in the spirit of her husband told me I was leading those girls down to Hell. Hell is the ever ready word in their mouths. The new head and bloody bones forever lifted to scare their neophytes into full submission.

We once more went up to the house and as many others did looked through the open windows. One young man, rather handsome, was kneeling before a young girl—his face close to hers *exhorting* her. Foote was addressing another in similar *tête à tête* in a corner of the room—and another, who was more desultory in his devotions, was walking from one to another. His eye met mine.

The power of these people like that of the animal magnetizer is neutralized if a sceptic is present. The youth passed and said to me, "You have been ordered off the ground. If you do not go, other measures will be taken." I replied very calmly that I understood the premises were Mr. Wetmore's, and if he requested it I should leave them. "If I were to kneel in that way before a maid," said our little expelled confessor, "I think I could give her some queer feelings." A fitting comment on the exhibition.

A conversation with a friend who had remarked that "there were three great things to be done—to be born—to marry—and to die—and to marry was the greatest for good and for evil" led Sedgwick to consider yet again her decision to remain unmarried. "I believe him," she had responded. Her reasons were telling.

23 May 1834: My constitutional timidity has perhaps had something to do with keeping me single, but if I had had the power to marry a man that I truly loved this would have been a slight hold back. I lately heard or read a remark that struck me—that romantic imaginative persons formed a beau ideal to which nothing in life approximated near enough to satisfy them. This may account for my never responding to the sentiments of those who sought me—though some of them certainly deserved more than I had to bestow—but I have seen those that I think I could have conjured into beau ideals.

The death of the Marquis de Lafayette led Sedgwick to reflect upon the meaning of "intellectual superiority." Insisting that such superiority was moral as well as mental, she applauded those whose intellect was dedicated to the betterment of humankind. Sedgwick's convictions aligned her with those who had made the practice of virtue the wellspring of intellectual (and social) superiority. Behavior, not affluence, determined status in this system. Not surprisingly, the system validated the particular elitism with which Sedgwick herself identified.

29 June 1834: We have received today the sad news of Lafayette's death. The friend of his own and of our country—but not of these

142

only—the friend of his race—the lover of mankind—the honest image after him who was the "express likening of the Divine being." And yet poor, weak, half-seeing men call him rather good than great! Is not such goodness as his the highest manifestation of Intellect? And is it not because Washington and Lafayette had attained to that most God-like quality *consistency* that his intellectual superiority is not obvious? Men look over a level and without noticing the elevation they think there is no height because one point does not rise above another. What is intellectual superiority? If a man in every variety of position and atmosphere discerns clearly and aright has he not a superior vision? How great is the change which his death makes to his survivors? How little to himself—for his were the purposes and affections of a Higher sphere. His walk has been with God. Oh, my country, may you never forget his services, never cease to profit by his example.

The English writer Harriet Martineau began her literary career with the publication of "Female Writers on Practical Divinity" in 1821, the year before Sedgwick's A New England Tale *appeared. When Martineau arrived in the United States thirteen years later, she and Sedgwick had secured national standing in their respective countries. Published in the early 1830s, Martineau's* Illustrations of Political Economy, *each of which celebrated classical economics, had brought her success. Sedgwick's subsequent novels had done the same. It was fitting, then, that Martineau spent four days in Stockbridge with Sedgwick and her relatives. Published in 1836, Martineau's controversial* Society in America *damned slavery as a betrayal of America's promise. A critic of slavery herself, Sedgwick agreed. Generally, however, she found the volume disappointing. The entry in her journal on 26 June 1837 noted that she had received a copy from Martineau. "I am sorry," she said, "for it puts me under the necessity of writing to her—looking at words and weighing phrases and all that dismal work—the worst sort of depreciation of currency when the heart refuses its stamp to the words. . . ."*

8 October [1834]: During the last week everything has been suspended by the great event of the Martineau's visit and when I intended to have made most records in my journal I have made none. I shall try now to set down my impression of this extraordinary woman who found us all strangers and left us friends. She arrived with her companion Miss [Louisa] Jeffrey and Mrs. Griffith last Thursday morning at 9. We expected her at the dinner hour and were just in the hurly burly of preparation. A sultry morning it was. I had undertaken to make some pies—rigged myself accordingly— drawn the table with the woodhouse—got all my matters well arranged when the ladies were announced.

Miss M. at first struck me as a plain woman with nothing in her face indicative of her splendid talents. She arranges her very dark brown hair (just beginning to grey) simply—her forehead is low— her nose short and thick—her mouth not well formed for she is *wapperjawed*[5] and her teeth so-so—rather pale and thin faced— tall and spare with *very* pretty hands and feet. She dresses with simplicity, economy, and great neatness. Her voice is so low as to be nearly inaudible at a little distance from her. Her deafness is not the barrier to intercourse with her which we feared, as she uses a long, flexible tube with a cup at one end into which you speak. She manages this so naturally and gracefully that after the novelty is over there is no embarrassment in talking with her—to most persons. Jane [Minot Sedgwick] said to her, "you have one advantage—no one will dare pour *folly* into this tube." "Oh," she said, "she flattered herself the great advantage was that it equalized her with the rest of the world— restored her to its follies, for who would be always wise." . . .

Miss M. told me that Dr. [William Ellery] Channing in a letter to Miss Aikin had said he feared her (Miss M.'s) impressions of the country would not be favorable—she would find the aspect of our people cold—she would be annoyed by the want of domestic comforts, and she would be shocked by filial insubordination. Miss M. said it was injudicious in him to give her any previous impression—

---

[5]"Wapperjawed" was the slang used to describe someone with a crooked jaw.

as it was. However, I think her mind is unbiased. Hers is not a mind to be governed by authority. . . . She was free from pedantry, display, assumingness, ostentation—all the infirmities of successful and flattered intellects, and this I take to be because her morale is pure and exalted. At first I thought a political economist was not the loveliest manifestation of woman—but from hour to hour she grew upon us—so modest, gentle, and kind, and before she went away we began to see the graces of her soul in her face as in a mirror.

On Friday, we went to the Shaker Villages, where they very grudgingly provided us some nice bread and butter.[6] I saw very little of Miss M. that day as Brother T[heodore] pretty much engrossed her. I rode in the wagon with her from Hancock to Lenox. She talked a good deal of Miss [Frances] Wright and of [Robert Dale] Owen.[7] She seemed to look on them both as a little wild, but not to think that either had, in their lives violated morality. She thinks that authors of opinions not yet established should not depart from the received usages of society unless their departure involves some painful effort or self-denial. For example, I presume she would have those who advance a less strict observance of the Sabbath than obtains in the religious world adhere to the established custom in practice while they preach against it, whereas if the opinion were in favor of more ascetic practice they should set the example. Miss M. thinks better of a licentious than an ascetic religion. The vices of the last are secret and hypocrisy is superadded to all the rest.

We took tea at Charles's [Sedgwick] and passed the evening en grande soirée at Susan's [Sedgwick], where the villagers again as-

[6]The Shakers, or the United Society of Believers in Christ's Second Appearing, as these millennial communitarians called themselves, established a series of communities in early 19th-century America. Numbering nearly 6,000 at the height of their popularity, the Shakers' communistic practices and their celibacy made them objects of curiosity. The Hancock Shaker Village that Martineau and Sedgwick visited was one of the largest communities.

[7]The British reformers Frances Wright (1795–1852) and Robert Dale Owen (1801–1877) were both participants in New Harmony, Indiana, an early 19th-century experiment in communitarianism founded by Owen's father. Together they edited the *New Harmony Gazette* and later the *Free Enquirer,* publications that promoted women's rights, universal education, and a more equal distribution of wealth.

sembled to observe and admire. Saturday it rained steadily and we had an indoors womanly day—no interruption or fear of it. Miss M. asked me when I began to write and what induced me to it. She seemed surprised and a little displeased with my want of frankness or rather communicativeness on the subject—said she liked to talk over her literary course (well she may!) and she had always found others so disposed. That "out of the abundance of the heart the mouth speaketh" and that it was impossible any one should be an author without having the matter deeply at heart. This is true and still it is true that in my case it is not affectation nor a parade of modesty, the worst of all parade. I have as much pleasure in success (and certainly as much in the *consciousness* of deserving it) as others. But I early took a disgust to hearing people talk of themselves— commonplace people, I suppose they were—besides my vanity forbids it. I see that most persons soon weary of listening to these self-glorifiers and self-expounders, or whatever they may be. We are in danger of self-exaggeration. The object that is nearest appears largest to the mental as well as the physical vision. I think too honestly it befits me to be modest. I have great defects of mind, partly resulting from my defective education and partly from my own self negligence, but I have wandered from my theme! . . .

Miss [Maria] E[dgeworth] is no favorite with Miss Martineau. She thinks her morality "very bad"—the foundation of all moral of her childrens' stories bad—the great motive upheld is opinion. . . .

In the evening [on Sunday] another gathering at Mr. Ashburner's. It was beautiful to see the deference paid to this rare union of genius and virtue. They formed a crescent in front of her three or four deep. I yielded my privilege to others and have nothing to record but the sentiment. Monday morning at half past six they left.

Beginning in the early 1820s, Sedgwick divided her year between New York City and Lenox, Massachusetts, where her brother Charles, his wife Elizabeth, and their children had settled. In describing how difficult it had been to part with their daughter Kate, Sedgwick made tangible the strength of her attachment to the child who bore her name.

146

Sedgwick's decision to remain unmarried made her all the more ready to construct strong and enduring relationships with her kin. More than any other niece or nephew, Kate stood in relation to Sedgwick as mother to child. Little wonder, then, that the prospect of separation gave her such pain. Upon Catharine's arrival in New York City she did acknowledge that Robert's and Elizabeth's children "made me feel that I had not left all happiness behind. These dear children are very near to me and go far to fill the aching void." Nonetheless, Sedgwick made the resolution penned at the end of this entry a reality—the next year Kate accompanied her aunt to New York City.

23 December 1834: Friday 12 was a sweet mild day. Saturday still mild snowing and clearing gently away in the evening. At dawn Sunday morning the weather changed. We went to S[tockbridge] after breakfast in a sleigh—Charles and Elizabeth, Kate and myself. It continued to grow cold till daylight Monday morning, when the mercury was 12 below cipher, having fallen more than 40 degrees in 24 hours.

Sunday was a *horrid* day to me—a day of unavailing regret and of slow torture. Monday morning came and my *guardian angel* decided I should not come—so after taking a few long breaths at the reprieve—enjoying a little—I again felt on the rack till Tuesday morning 16, when I was swung off! The truth is I have not courage for these awful partings and I think I shall never subject myself again to such unnecessary suffering. I shall not again voluntarily part from my Kate. My heart has grown *fast to her.* I could just bear to go away if she were with me. I feel too my love growing stronger to the country and to country life.

On the day after her forty-fifth birthday, Sedgwick considered the relative importance of her highly successful career and her intimate relationships. That she privileged the latter suggests less a diminished commitment to her career than the desire of a woman who was putatively alone for sustained connections with others.

29 December 1834: I have passed my birthday. I am *forty five years old*—descending into the vale of life. I have lived beyond the average term of human life. I have enjoyed much. I have suffered. But for the most part I can look back upon a very happy life. I have reason to bless God for his tender mercies. My path has been sometimes in safety when it would have been far otherwise if I had marked it. I have enjoyed far more of the world's respect than I ever expected, or I believe I can honestly say, care for—any further than I may make it subservient to my usefulness. My dearest profession is the love of my friends—that the moth and rust of time [has] not consumed. In some instance a portion of what was mine has been diverted into other channels, and if my heart has ached and *does ache* at this, I do not repine and will not be exacting. Enough is mine—and I devoutly thank God, for I could not live without it. The tender love of the young ones is mine and that is bathing my old limbs in the pool of Bethesda. My prayer and desire now is to spend the time that remains to me for the good of others, for their good and happiness and to be prepared by faithful service for the summons of my master.

After she had traveled through the South and the West, Harriet Martineau returned to Stockbridge for a second visit. Sedgwick used the occasion to consider the reasons for Martineau's prominence relative to other literary Englishwomen of her generation. It is telling that Sedgwick did not have American contemporaries with whom she could compare herself. In contrast to Martineau, Sedgwick stood nearly alone in her nation as a prominent writer who happened to be a woman.

9 August 1835: No woman has ever, perhaps, received so rich a recompense of reward— and why? I think because her spirit and influence have been in harmony with the spirit of the age—because she has gone with the current. She has devoted God's good gifts to the use of his creatures. Other women have shown as powerful a genius as hers. Mrs. Barbauld, I think superior—Miss Edgeworth

more various talents and a fuller demonstration—Mrs. Somerville higher attainments in science—Mrs. Hemans a more exquisite gift in the loftiest department of imagination—and Mrs. Jameson a more general cultivation, a richer imagination, and the power of embodying her own rich thoughts in a more poetic—more drawing room—if not as vigorous a style.[8] But Miss M. with a single eye to general good has, with the light of philosophy and religion on her path, devoted herself not to the intellectual amusement or advancement of the gifted and educated, but to make bread more plentiful in the husbandman's dwelling, and to still the cry of hunger forever in the poor man's cottage—and with the bread that perisheth to give him that which cometh down from Heaven. It is this that makes us all cry her Hail thou favored among women! . . . She seldom speaks unless addressed, but in reply to a single touch she pours out a rich stream. She is never brilliant—never says a thing that is engraven on or *cut in* to your memory but she talks on a greater variety of topics than any one I ever heard agreeably, most agreeably and with sense and information. She is *womanly*—strictly with sympathies fresh from the heart—enthusiasms not always *manifestly* supported by reason—now and then *bordering* on the dogmatical, but too thorough a love of human rights ever I think to overstep the boundary and she is I think not conceited—no, not in the least, but quite aware of her own superiority and perhaps a little too frank on this point.

In a letter written in January 1834, the Reverend Henry Ware, Jr., a fellow Unitarian, invited Sedgwick to contribute to a series of volumes "offering to the public an exhibition of the practical character and influences of Christianity." Ware suggested an experimental form different from any Sedgwick had attempted—a narrative that stood "between a formal tale and a common tract." Published in 1835, Home:

---

[8]In addition to the writers Anna Letitia Aikin Barbauld (1743–1825), Maria Edgeworth (1767–1849), and Anna Jameson (1794–1860), Sedgwick cited as examples the poet Felicia Hemans (1793–1835) and the scientist Mary Somerville (1780-1872).

Scenes and Characters Illustrating Christian Truth *did exactly that,*
as did The Poor Rich Man and the Rich Poor Man *(1836),* Live and
Let Live *(1837), and* Means and Ends *(1839). The highly favorable*
reception to Home *that Sedgwick recorded in the following entries was*
surely an important factor in the appearance of these volumes in such
rapid succession. Sedgwick had met with the educator and reformer
Elizabeth Peabody during a visit to Boston in the autumn of 1835. The
mill girl's observations provided by Peabody obviously gratified her.
Sedgwick encountered the strangers who praised Home *when she*
stopped briefly in Worcester while enroute to Lenox and Stockbridge.
Sedgwick's third entry about the laudatory response to Home *was*
made in New York City shortly after she had arrived there for the
winter.

11 November 1835: Miss Peabody called in the P.M. Miss P. gratified
me very much with the testimony of an intelligent, *orthodox* factory
girl about *Home.* She said if they would spend their Sundays in
Lowell, as recommended in this book, how much good might be
done. This is better than the opinion of half the ministers in New
England. She said a gentleman had said to her, "I must go home
and read *The Linwoods.* It takes me half an hour to read a page. I
should as soon think of galloping through Paradise." I like to save
up these bonbons when they are so very sweet.

20 November 1835: We passed a pleasant evening at Worcester.
While I was awaiting tea with a stranger and his wife, the lady asked
me if I had read Miss Sedgwick's *Home?* "Yes." "Don't you think it's
beautiful?" I smiled and said I did not know. "Don't you?" (most
emphatically) "Well my husband and I think it most beautiful." "I
have not yet read Miss S.'s last work," said the husband, "but it's
spoken very highly of." Some other question was asked, and I
thought it but decent to declare myself, whereupon the lady expressed the utmost delight at meeting me.

17 December 1835: I have met everyone with congratulations about
my book, which has, I think, proved more generally acceptable than

anything I have before written. My *author's* existence has always seemed something accidental, extraneous, and independent of my inner self. My books have been a pleasant occupation and excitement in my life. The notice and friends or acquaintances they have procured me have relieved me from the danger of ennui and blue devils that are most apt to infect a single person. But they constitute no portion of my happiness—that is of such as I derive from the dearest relations of life. When I feel that my writings have made anyone happier or better I feel an emotion of gratitude to Him who has made me the medium of any blessing to my fellow creatures. And I do feel that I am but the instrument.

The death of a former suitor led Sedgwick to reflect upon the choice she had made about marriage. Whatever loneliness she had suffered, whatever pain her secondary status had entailed, William Jarvis's death reminded Sedgwick of her conviction that a successful marriage required much more than the "liking" she had felt for the then "young man of five and twenty." Sedgwick's circumstances had been more fortunate than many of her contemporaries. Financial independence had made the choice possible. Devoted siblings had relieved the isolation. Nonetheless, Sedgwick's scrupulous honesty in her relations with Jarvis remains striking.

12 October 1836: Charles sent me on Saturday night the news of William Jarvis's death. He shot himself through the heart. I remember him [as] a young man, five and twenty when I first knew him. His head had then a striking beauty. His complexion was clear, brilliant, English; his eyes prominent, deep blue, and full of humor and pure as a child's; his mouth beautiful; his person clumsy, and gait shuffling, or rather hitchy. He was ambitious, proud, social, kindhearted, and a lover of wit, rather than witty himself. It seems to me that I can now hear his chuckling laugh at some good thing of *Harry's*—or some playfulness of Charles. He became a lover of mine. At his first declaration I refused him, but I liked him, and not knowing quite as much of the heart (or of *my* heart) as I now do I

fancied that liking might ripen into something warmer. Harry was his and my confidant, and influenced by his advice and Jarvis's entreaties I consented the affair should remain open while I passed the winter in New York. He wrote to me often by my consent on the condition his letters should be mere letters of friendship. I never answered them. I found from week to week that like all feeble attachments mine was dying away under absence, and finally impelled by a dream I wrote him a finale. I had dreamed that the wedding day was come, that I was filled with horror but thought it too late to recede. My family were assembled. We were standing up, and Dr. West had begun the ceremony when making a last effort, I begged him to stop and turning to Jarvis said, "I cannot marry you. I do not love you!" He looked at me far more in sorrow than in anger. I shall never forget the expression and said, "You should have told me this before!" Immediately after receiving my letter he went to Pittsfield and married a few months [later]—a commonplace girl—a *poor thing*. How much this marriage may have affected his character no one can tell. A man of right character would never have made it—poor fellow! I remember after a long walk in which we had much talk, rather unsatisfactory, he concluded, "well it will be all the same a hundred years hence!" I smiled then and have many a time since as it occurred [to me], but since this last scene of his drama I have thought, "will it be the same—to either of us?" I am more and more a fatalist. Events control us—not we events.

Little more than a year after William Jarvis's death had occasioned her meditation on marriage, Sedgwick returned to a familiar subject—her relationship with her siblings. She insisted that she was fortunate, as indeed she was. But that enduring desire still to be primary in the lives of those who had committed themselves to others left her dissatisfied. Here too Sedgwick's honesty about the costs of "single life" is placed in sharp relief, as is her devotion to her siblings.

2 December 1837: Anxious as I am to avoid those "jealous creepings of nature" that are so apt to infect us as we go on in life, I cannot

altogether. Moth and rust do attack our affections which should be incorruptible. It is the chief misery of single life, its keenest suffering, that the sister in early life, the object of fondest love, of partial exaggerating love, must yield her place to one and another till she begins to perceive the transformation of affection to duty and at last that poor, cold substitute is sometimes forgotten. I can say with truth that the flattery, the praise, the fame, if it may have that grand name, which have attended my later years, have been no compensation for the gradual drying away of the sweet fountains of nature. Perhaps there never was a being that had less to complain of in this way than myself and a great portion of my suffering results doubtless from the overweening indulgence of my early years. Charles, if he loves others better than me, loves me as he loves no one else. With him I am *satisfied*. I use this word because it is the *strongest* that with my unreasonable cravings I can use. Jane [Minot Sedgwick] is more than a sister—my elected closest, dearest friend. From the love of these two there is no power, no influence, no, not my own unworthiness [that] can separate me. [Sister] Frances loves everything and me with the rest with an unmeasured love. I think Brother Theodore loves me better than when we were young. The difference in our ages then separated us, and his affections have become more diffused and stronger as he has grown older. Susan [Ridley Sedgwick] has been a most steadfast friend—unfailing in every act of kindness. [Her daughter] Maria has naturally and inevitably taken the place I once held to her. I think she does not love me less, but the habits of our intercourse are less intimate. I am sure that every year—[every] day gives me more reason to honor and love her. [Charles's wife] Elizabeth is invariably affectionate, generous, and kind. [Robert's wife] Lizzy has been very kind and affectionate in her conduct to me. [The next sentences have been carefully inked out. In the margin alongside the passage, Sedgwick wrote on 24 July 1846.] Here I had written a lamentation over the transference of the first place in my dear brother Robert's heart. He had been father, lover as well as brother to me, and when in the inevitable concentration of a closer tie I felt an aching void, I expressed it as I should not. Years passed on and I had proof that the love of our early years for a time without its usual demonstrations was there in that tenderest of hearts. Now after *five* years of separation from him I daily, almost hourly, mourn him. He is actual presence to me.

In saying farewell to Anna Jameson, Sedgwick marveled at the intimacy that had been so quickly established between them. She and Jameson, as Sedgwick noted in the second volume of her autobiography, maintained their friendship until the latter's death in 1860.

10 February 1838: [Anna Jameson] embarked on board the *Quebec* for London. I have parted with her with more sorrow than I believed I could have felt at parting with a person whom I have known but—I must think how long for it seems to me as if years instead of months had flowed over our acquaintance. It is just three months and seven days since I first saw her. I feel grateful to her for her warm, unmeasured, and unexpected affection for me. I cannot account for it but by the hypothesis that she had love pent up in her heart ready to place upon the first person that could stir the water of the fountain.

Early in 1838 Sedgwick's brother Robert suffered a stroke that left him permanently disabled. Sedgwick became his main caretaker. An unmistakable mark of her devotion, this charge returned them to a relationship in which Sedgwick was primary in Robert's life.

21 April [1838]: Never did I live a busier life, nor in some respects a more satisfactory [one]. *Every* moment of my time is occupied. I have not to select—to say I will do this this hour—and that the next—but my work is before me and I must push through it, and that work is to discharge the thousand little household duties and to make Robert as comfortable as I can by anticipating his little wants and performing a thousand nameless services, insignificant in themselves but important to him. I wash him, I read to him, I

walk with him, and I have the inexpressible happiness of feeling that I am useful to him.

In the spring of 1839, Sedgwick and her niece Kate accompanied Robert and his family on a fifteen-month journey to Europe. Everyone hoped that traveling would promote Robert's recovery. Unfortunately, his condition continued to deteriorate and he died little more than a year after their return. It was fitting that Sedgwick devoted the final passage in this volume of her journal to a description of the last hours before her departure. She spent those hours with Charles, another brother who was equally important to her.

7 April [1839]: I came to New York with my dear Charles on Wednesday 12 March. He remained here till Sunday [the] 30th. Every hour is precious with him. Shall we again meet in the places where we have lived, felt—

Almost exactly a decade later, Sedgwick made the initial entry in the last volume of her journal. Discontinuity, change, and loss had marked her personal relationships during the intervening years. Robert's death in September 1841 had made her "feel as if half my life were buried in his grave." Charles was now the only brother who remained. Kate had married William Minot one year later. Initially, Sedgwick had been devastated—shortly after Kate and William were engaged, she told Anna Jameson that "when her lover came like a thief in the night and got her vows plighted to him, I took to my bed and cried my eyes almost out, and behaved, in short, like a fool." But as this entry shows, she found yet another home with Kate, William, and their children, Alice and William III, all of whom she "enjoyed more than volumes can tell." Born in 1847, Kate's daughter Alice, the autobiography's putative reader, became Sedgwick's particular delight. The trajectory of Sedgwick's literary career had remained the same throughout the decade, although she no longer employed the form of tale cum tract that had characterized Home, The Poor Rich Man and the Rich Poor Man, Live and Let Live, *and* Means and Ends. *Turning instead to a more familiar approach, she published tales and sketches in the nation's leading periodicals. Entitled* Letters From Abroad, *the journal she had kept while traveling in Europe appeared in 1841.*

30 June 1849: I came on the twelfth of this month of June 1849 to Woodbourne and in spite of cold when we kept fires and reposed by them all day—and heat when the mercury day and night ranged between seventy-five and ninety-six in Kate's *cool* parlor, I have passed the time most tranquilly blessed with the sight of my beloved Kate, with a growing love for her husband, and with the unmeasured kindness of all his people—and (I must not say above all) with my darling little Alice. We have walked together—told stories—had our little tête à tête tea parties—played dolls, and in short had all sorts of socialities befitting contemporaries.

In this entry Sedgwick returned to a subject that echoed through the journal—the decision she had made to remain unmarried. She still believed the choice had been the appropriate one, although she now believed that she should have established a household separate from her siblings and their families. Sedgwick did not elaborate upon the reasons for her decision in this entry. Instead, she made her singular position the subject of her last novel, the aptly titled Married or Single?

16 July 1849: [In deciding not to establish a household,] I was chiefly deterred by my very limited means—but I might have done it—I might have had my industry more directed to the enlargement of my fortune and the little income that has gone like dew might have told in one channel. It is past. But one opinion is the result of my experience—and I suspect no single woman living the household of others has been happier—yet I would advise every woman who can, by any effort, secure an independent home to have it. She will increase tenfold her means of doing good. She will avoid dangers and irritations and perchance save heartaches that the world never knows or suspects.

More than fifteen years after she published Home *in 1835, Sedgwick received the letter which she describes in this entry. Validating as it did the literary experiment Sedgwick had undertaken in a tale that was simultaneously a tract, the physician's praise meant much to her. Her reaction also suggested that the career she was now concluding had played a signal role in shaping her self-definition. Sedgwick published her last novel in 1857, six years after she had made this entry.*

5 December 1851: Woodbourne. I came here three weeks since on 14 November. Last summer I received a letter from a Doctor Cummings of Fitzwilliam, New Hampshire. His letter informed me that he had *discovered* my *Home*—and since that he had procured as many of my writings as he could obtain. He wrote to me for a complete list. His letter expressed with the simplicity and earnestness of a man accustomed to a fact-life a very hearty admiration of what he had read and a strong desire for more. I answered and offered if he would direct the mode to send him *Hope Leslie*—in reply he begged me to forward it by mail and enclosed a dollar Bank note to defray the expense. Subsequently he wrote very modestly proposing to "call on me at Lenox" and wished me to appoint the time. I did. He was prevented by illness among his patients and finally after I came here a letter was forwarded from Lenox.

Consistent in tone and content with Sedgwick's earlier reflections upon a life that was filled with complexity, this final entry in her journal illustrates a persistent self-deprecation. What she left unremarked were the substantial achievements of a woman who committed herself to both a professional career and a large number of personal relationships in which she displayed an exceptional capacity for generous and sympathetic intimacy. Sedgwick's already familiar longing for primacy in the lives of her brothers is apparent in this entry. But now she was able to acknowledge that this desire was at least partially relieved by the profound connection she had established with her niece Kate. Thirteen years after she made this entry, Sedgwick died at Woodbourne, the residence that Kate shared with her husband and children.

28 December 1854: This is my birthday—cloudy, leaden, and drizzling, typifying the state of my spirits this day—and yet what reasons have I for thankfulness, for the mercies that have followed my whole life—from the cradle to this, the last stage of my pilgrimage. In possession of health and strength, it is difficult for me to realize how old I am—how near the end. I look forward calmly, for I throw myself on the *mercy* of God—on the patience and infinite tenderness of Jesus—but truly I am overwhelmed with a sense of my *poor* life—of my neglect of gifts—abuse and neglect of opportunities—of my self-indulgence. Religion has not overcome the evil in me—the unspirituality—the levity—the coldness—the imperfect faith and trust—the fear and dread—the levity and vanity and dissatisfactions. Oh God be merciful to me. I feel so acutely—so unworthily the inevitable change from the time when I was first in many hearts to being first in none and though I have much more affection and consideration than falls to the lot of many at my age, yet there is more of that spontaneous, ever-present, caressing love that petted me and spoiled except—except those dear little children. How strangely exacting should I appear to some others—God knows I do not envy others of our household—but who can see the dreariness that brings tears to my eyes from a world of memories and mourning—who guesses. Someone turns to me and says, "you are not well today," and I answer as of course, "not very well," but oh the sickness of the heart. God forgive me. I ought only to be thankful and contented—hopeful and knowing that I ought and am not is my misery. But here I am with my sweet Kate—who is most filial—most satisfactory—and William who is more than I could ask or ever hoped or expected her husband could be and their lovely and most beloved children. Oh my soul and all that is within me praise my God and Father.

Index

Adams, Hannah, CMS visits, 115; reads J. Milton, 116
Adams, Henry, 5
African Americans, 15–17, and social barriers, 32
Agrippa, 68–69, 87
Aix-la-Chapelle, Treaty of, 46n.
Albany, N.Y., CMS attends school, 20, 104–106; E. S. Pomeroy moves to, 88, Pomeroy family home, 121–122; CMS visits, 88, 110
Andrews, Caroline (Tucker), 115
Ashburner, Sarah, 139, 140, 141
Autobiography, approaches to, 5–6
Autun, Bishop of, 62

Backus, Azel, 88
Baillie, Joanna, 109
Banner, James M., Jr., 8n.
Barbaud, Anna, 22, 35, 83, 148
Baxter, Miss, 105
Beecher, Henry Ward, 96
Bell, Mrs., 132, school, 20, 94, 100, 104–106
Bell, Susan Groag, 5n.
Bellamy, Joseph, 54, 55
Bennington, Vt., political parties, 9–10, 81; CMS attends school, 20; CMS visits, 80–82
Bentley's Miscellany, 17
Bernard, Richard, 19n.
Berquin, Arnaud, 22, 82–83
Bleecker, Harmanus, 110

Bludgruddery, Dennis, 56
Borgia, Caesar, 121
Boston, Mass., CMS attends school, 21
Bradstreet, Anne, 5–6
Brogan, Billy, 51
Brooke, Henry, 104n.
Brown, Elsa Barkley, 16n.
Brown, Richard D., 31n.
Bryant, William Cullen, 4, 56, 119, obituary of A. Jameson, 106–107
Buell, Lawrence, 32n.
Butler, Pierce, 132
Butler, Samuel, 74
Byron, Harriet, 48n.

Calvinism, 36–37, 86, 88, 95–96, 122, 138–142
Canandaigua, N.Y., CMS visits, 110–111
Cape Breton Island, N.S., 46
Careers, and women, 22
Catholicism, in Stockbridge, 50–52
Cato, 110
Cavendish, Margaret, 5
Cervantes Saavedra, Miguel de, 21, 74
Channing, William Ellery, 31, 32, 119, 144
Charvat, William, 32n.
Churchill, Mr., 140
Clap, Thomas, 54n.
Clarence. See Catharine Maria Sedgwick, *Clarence*.
Class, and education, 19; and social responsibility, 31–33
Cooper, James Fenimore, 4, 119

INDEX

Hope Leslie. See Catharine Maria Sedgwick, *Hope Leslie.*
Hopkins, Electa (Sergeant), 49
Hopkins, Mark (1739–1776), 54, 55
Hopkins, Mark (1802–1887), 49, 54
Howe, Daniel Walker, 32n.
Hume, David, 21, 74

Iliad, 101–102
Ingersoll, Mrs., and Catholicism, 50–51
Irish, CMS on, 50–53
Irving, Washington, 4, 119

Jackson, Andrew, CMS visits, 128–129
Jamaica, R. Sedgwick expedition, 45
Jameson, Anna, 35, 108, 149, 155, death, 100, 111, obituary by W. C. Bryant, 106–107; failed marriage, 107; character, 107–108; and R. Sedgwick, 108; Sedgwicks visit, 108–110; visits CMS, 154
Jarvis, William, 28–29, 151–152
Jefferson, Thomas, and French influence, 64
Jeffrey, Louisa, 144
Julian of Norwich, Dame, 5

Kelley, Mary, 31n.
Kemble, Frances Anne ("Fanny"), 109–110, 111, 132–133, adapts CMS anecdote, 84, 87
Kempe, Margery, 5
Kerber, Linda K., 8n., 11n.
King George's War, 46
Kingsley, Charles, 104
Kinne, Aaron, 98
Knox, Vicesimus, 83n.
Kosciuszko, Tadeusz, 68–69

Lady Prime, 68
Lafayette, Marquis de, 142–143
"Lafayettism," 33, 118, 119
Lalliet, M., 73, 90
Lamb, Charles, 102
Ledyard, Benjamin, 90n.
Ledyard, Susan (Livingston), 90, 93
Legal profession, 79
Letters From Abroad. See Catharine Maria Sedgwick, *Letters From Abroad.*
Lewis, Jan, 11n.

Liancourt, duc de, 61–62
Linwoods. See Catharine Maria Sedgwick, *Linwoods.*
Live and Let Live. See Catharine Maria Sedgwick, *Live and Let Live.*
Livingston, Henry Brockholst, 90, 93
Louisbourg, N.S., 46n.
Lynch, Lawrence, 50

Macbeth, CMS attends, 91
MacEacheren, Elaine, 17n.
Machiavelli, Niccolo, CMS reads *Prince,* 120–121
Marriage, 11–15, 18–19, and coverture, 10; and CMS, 22, 27–28, 29, 122–123, 127, 147; and gender, 23, 24; divorce, 23; requirements, 29; CMS on, 38–39, 142, 151–154, 156; deference in, 58–59
Married or Single? See Catharine Maria Sedgwick, *Married or Single?*
Marshall, John, visits CMS, 128
Martineau, Harriet, 34–35, visits CMS, 143–146, 148–149
Mason, Jeremiah, 56
Mason, John, 56n.
Mason, John Mitchell, preaches in Stockbridge, 99
Mason, Mary, 6n.
Massachusetts, and slavery, 16–17, 124–126
Means and Ends. See Catharine Maria Sedgwick, *Means and Ends.*
Mental health, 13–14, 25–26, 59–60, 62–63, 89n., 124
Milton, John, 65, 102, 139, H. Adams reads, 116
Minot, Alice, 3, 6, 15, 94, 155, 156, and CMS autobiography, 45
Minot, Katharine ("Kate") (Sedgwick), 3, 94, 123, 130, 146–147, 156, 157, 158, European trip, 155; marriage, 155
Minot, Louisa, 24, 31
Minot, William, 39, 94, 156, 157, 158, and CMS autobiography, 3, 45; marriage, 155
Minot, William III, 94, 155
Mohawks, attack feared, 49–50
Morton, Jacob, CMS dines with, 92
Mumbet. See Elizabeth Freeman ("Mumbet").

INDEX